JEROME

Solving the Mystery of Nova Scotia's Silent Castaway

Fraser Mooney Jr.

NIMBUS
PUBLISHING

Nimbus Publishing Limited
PO Box 9166, Halifax, NS B3K 5M8
(902) 455-4286 www.nimbus.ca

Printed and bound in Canada
Nimbus Publishing is committed to protecting our natural environment. As part of our efforts, this book is printed on 100% recycled content stock.

Design: John van der Woude

Library and Archives Canada Cataloguing in Publication

Mooney, Fraser
Jerome : solving the mystery of Nova Scotia's
silent castaway / Fraser Mooney.
Includes bibliographical references.
ISBN 978-1-55109-686-5

1. Jerome, ca. 1843-1912. 2. Castaways—Nova Scotia Biography. 3. Mute persons—Nova Scotia—Biography. 4. Amputees—Nova Scotia—Biography. 5. Saint Marys Bay Region (N.S.)—Biography. 6. Saint Marys Bay Region (N.S.)—History. I. Title.

FC2345.S24Z49 2008   971.6'3202092   C2008-904608-0

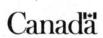

We acknowledge the financial support of the Government of Canada through the Book Publishing Industry Development Program (BPIDP) and the Canada Council, and of the Province of Nova Scotia through the Department of Tourism, Culture and Heritage for our publishing activities.

This book is dedicated to my biggest fans:
Mom, Dad, Phil, Allison, Elaine, Leone, and Marilyn.
And to Melanie, Lydia, and Madeline, I am your biggest fan.

Jerome...please forgive the intrusion.

Table of Contents

Preface

Jerome would hate this book. I don't take it personally, because I know Jerome would have hated the countless newspaper and magazine articles written about him, as well as the plays, the movie, and even the website. He was a man who simply wanted to be left alone, yet for most of his life he was the centre of attention. Unfortunately for the shy Jerome, he remains a fascinating character with a compelling story.

Before his death in 1912, Jerome was the most famous anonymous man in the world—a silent, sphinx-like human puzzle living among the Acadian people along the French Shore of St. Mary's

Bay. Poets, playwrights, and politicians; journalists and jurists; cartoonists and filmmakers have all taken turns interpreting the mystery-shrouded life of Jerome. The curiosity surrounding his life continued long after his death—since you are reading this book, it seems the curiosity still exists.

Like many people from southwestern Nova Scotia, I had heard the name Jerome as a youngster and was vaguely aware he was a mysterious, injured castaway who lived in Clare. I only became fascinated with the mystery of Jerome when I was working as a commercial writer for Radio CLJS in Yarmouth. It was 1994, and filmmaker Phil Comeau's acclaimed movie *Le Secret de Jérôme* was a blockbuster at our local theatre. Jerome-mania swept southwestern Nova Scotia. With a huge hit movie about a local legend playing to sellout crowds, I got to thinking about possible radio ad spinoffs for CLJS. I composed several trial radio commercials featuring a Jerome theme. Thankfully, my quirky Jerome spots never aired. In hindsight, the idea was not very clever or respectful. I only came to discover how disrespectful the cancelled radio spots were when I got to know Jerome better. But Jerome would not allow me to get to know him easily.

My failed attempts at making Jerome a radio pitchman made me realize how little I knew about his story. To satisfy my growing interest in the mystery, I visited the Yarmouth library, but was only able to find a couple of brief references to Jerome in books about Digby County. I was somewhat disappointed, but also intrigued that so few details were easily accessible about such a legendary figure. The facts that I did find often contradicted one another. So I began a bit of a quest, collecting whatever information I could about Jerome, and speaking to people with ties to Saint Alphonse, Clare, and Digby Neck.

I never thought I would accumulate enough research to justify a full-length book. But Jerome surprised me. He surprised me a lot. After filling several notebooks with research, I realized there was much more information than I had anticipated. The thought of devoting an entire book to Jerome didn't seem so absurd. While my friends and family certainly encouraged my research, they were less enthusiastic about my plans for a book.

"It's been done before," was the reply I often got when I mentioned my idea. But it hadn't. Over the years, many chapters have been written about Jerome, but in all my research I never found an entire book on the subject. The legend of Jerome was so pervasive that people just assumed a book had been done before. Regardless, I certainly felt I had something fresh to say.

There was more to write, if only to try to clear up the countless inconsistencies in the story. The details differ depending on which source you consult, or which local storyteller you speak with. Unfortunately many of the available sources are contradictory, and contain incorrect dates and names. Too often, especially in the case of newspaper articles, information has been lifted, sometimes word for word, from earlier published pieces. I tried to evaluate all of this information and make the best conclusions possible. I've had to make some guesses and indulge in some speculation about certain aspects of this story, but these instances should be clear to the reader. I have attempted to sort through all of the facts, conspiracies, and theories, and have woven all of the elements into a compelling story.

Jerome is the book I wish was available when I first became interested in the story. This book not only examines the central mystery of who Jerome was and where he came from, but also explores the lives and motivations of the many interesting Nova Scotians who cared for the castaway.

The good news for mystery lovers is that this book does not contain all of the answers. There is still plenty of mystery left to wring from the story of Jerome. The last word is still to be written. And when the last word is finally published, Jerome will hate that too.

Acknowledgements

To my patient wife Melanie's frustration, I often said this book was never going to write itself. That was my excuse to sit in front of the computer instead of helping with the lawn work, home repairs, painting, etc. Thankfully, along with the support of my wife, I have received plenty of advice and encouragement throughout the many years I have been working on this project.

For the many people who have offered guidance, information, and inspiration, I offer my most sincere thanks. This book would not have been possible without you. Please be assured that all errors in fact or inference—and there are sure to be some—are mine and mine alone.

To all those who offered encouragement, direction, and advice, I am extremely grateful. Special thanks go to my friend Matthew Trask, for the use of the laptop and the honest opinions. I also need to thank:

Charles Armour, whom I had the pleasure to meet one morning at the Dalhousie University Archives; Caley Baker; John Barham; Chris Bavis; Sally Blenkhorn; Eva Boudreau; Caroline-Isabel Caron; Pam Ciccarelli for helping me with my Italian; Rose Clements of South West Health Library Services; Cecil Comeau; Darlene Comeau-Mooney; Edith Comeau-Tufts; Victor Comeau; Sandy Cook of the Nova Scotia Legislative Library; Marie Cox; Kathleen D'Entremont-Mooney; Pierre Ferron; Brian Flemming, columnist with the defunct Halifax Daily News; Dave Gunning; Dave Hall; Lucy Jardine, New Brunswick Public Archives; Doris Landry; Louise Le Pierres, the Chronicle-Herald Library; Jackie MacDonald, South West Health Library Services, for telling me about Fog Magic; Ami MacKay; Stewart MacLean; Dianne Marshall; Sandra McIntyre; Paul Melanson; Memorial University of Newfoundland Archives staff; Pam Menchenton; David Mooney for your incredible story and spirit; Marven Moore and the staff of the Maritime Museum of the Atlantic; Margaret Murphy and the rest of the Nova Scotia Legislative Library staff; Sarah Naish of Queens County Historical

Society; Royce Nixon; MaryAnn Parnell and the current staff of Yarmouth Branch of Western Counties Regional Library; Katie Perkins; Sandra Phinney; Public Archives of New Brunswick staff; Lynn-Marie Richard; Lise Robichaud; Eric Ruff; Jason Saulnier of Centre Acadien; Carol Sherman; Gary Shutlak and the staff of Nova Scotia Public Archives; Blair Titus; Michelle Trask; Kevin Vallillee for turning me on to the Prince of Pictou; Aunt Ellen Webster; and Ray Zinck.

Chapter 1

The Hermit

Like a bony, broken finger, Digby Neck and its islands poke out into the Bay of Fundy, pointing west toward the Gulf of Maine. The skinny finger of craggy land—over forty kilometres long but barely five kilometres wide—seems to beckon sailors and ships, urging them to sail closer and embrace its rocky coast. Such an invitation has been difficult to resist over the years and many ships have been dashed against the shores of Digby Neck, flinging desperate sailors onto its beaches.

One beach on the long spit of land seems like it should be exempt from such unsettling events as shipwrecks. Sandy Cove has all the attributes of a safe haven. The dramatic rocky peak of Mount Shubel overlooks and protects the charming village of Sandy Cove and its lovely round harbour, which is enclosed on almost all sides by a ring of tree-covered hills. With its narrow mouth opening into St. Mary's Bay, the harbour of Sandy Cove looks like it has been taken directly from the pages of a storybook. The uniqueness of the area inspired Nova Scotia travel writer Clara Dennis to comment in her book *Down in Nova Scotia* that its "beauty and grandeur rends it a place for poets' dreams."

Travellers almost always pause to enjoy the striking scenery at Sandy Cove, located halfway down the neck at its narrowest spot. The village sits between two bays—a sheltered harbour on the St. Mary's Bay side and a wider, crescent-shaped, sand-covered cove on the Bay of Fundy side.

Like countless coastal communities, the shore of Digby Neck has its own cast of colourful characters. A man the people called George Coll, or Collie, was just such a character. He was born in 1855 and became known as the Hermit of Sandy Cove after living alone for many years on the fringes of the small village.

Some villagers may have regarded Collie with affection, but he was likely avoided and shunned by most. They pointed and laughed behind the back of the strange man as he left his rundown shack on his way to the beach to dig clams at low tide. His odd behaviour and shabby clothes made him a favourite target for local children who amused themselves at his expense. Collie seemed to enjoy the attention he received from them, and could often be bribed into putting on a little show in exchange for bits of bread, biscuits, and other treats.

Visitors to Digby Neck who heard rumours of the Hermit of Sandy Cove would sometimes seek out Old Collie. Although he preferred to be left alone, he had a fondness for tobacco—especially certain American brands—and would gladly accept it as a gift from his guests. After passing him the tobacco, his visitors would join him for a smoke while trying to coax a story or two out of the Hermit. Old Collie could tell many tales if he was in good humour. The tale most visitors to the shack wanted to hear was a mystery story that began when Collie was just a boy.

"Tell the story of how you found the man on the beach," was a request put to the Hermit many, many times.

After hearing the question, Collie probably scratched his whiskered chin and gazed out toward the beach he had walked on nearly every day since he learned to stand on two feet. And if Collie were in the mood to talk, he would tell the story of his accidental discovery of a stranger on the Sandy Cove beach, an event that marked the beginning of one of the most enduring mysteries in Maritime lore.

In the summer of 1863, George Colin Albright was a curious lad only eight years old. The boy was nicknamed Collie so that he would not be confused with his father, a poor fisherman after whom he was named.

Even though they were hard-working, the Albright family was looked down upon by the villagers of Sandy Cove. The finer, sturdier homes of the village were a sharp contrast to the family's shack on the edge of the beach. Later newspaper stories unkindly described the Albrights as a "half-witted family" that camped out at the high-water mark.

Life on the bay was all the education the Albright children had or needed. Very little happened on the beach at Sandy Cove without young George Colin Albright being aware of it—and going to investigate. It was during such an investigation on September 8, 1863, that he made a remarkable discovery.

It was early morning, just as the sun was rising and the morning haze was lifting from the beach. The tide was out, leaving the entire beach in full view. It had rained the night before—a cold rain—leaving the area even more damp and soggy than usual. Young Collie and his older brother William, who was ten at the time, could scan the entire length of the beach from the front door of their family's small house. From their vantage point, they likely saw the usual flotsam and jetsam of driftwood, seaweed, and discarded fishing gear strewn about the sand.

One of the boys pointed to a large rock halfway down the beach near the high-water mark. The boulder usually stuck out of the water at high tide, but since the tide was down the entire stone was exposed. They spotted an unfamiliar dark object near the rock, either leaning against it or perched upon it. At first they assumed it was a seal—but as they watched it, they became less certain. Seals did not usually stay at the high-water mark for long when the tide was out. The boys became very curious about this mysterious creature and went to take a closer look.

The Albrights' shack was built on the top of the bank that led to the beach, so Collie and William simply scrambled down the hill to reach the sand. As they got closer to the object near the rock, the boys were shocked to discover it was no seal at all. It was a man.

The stranger was ghostly pale and deathly still. The boys probably believed the motionless man, who was likely the victim of a shipwreck, was dead. As Collie and William crept even closer, they noticed something was not quite right with the man's lifeless body. He was not all there. He was missing something. The stranger had no legs.

Bewildered by this discovery, the boys may have grabbed a piece of driftwood to poke the body. A moan or a movement from him let the Albright boys know the strange, legless man was still alive… but barely.

It is not known if the boys tried to talk to the stranger. It is more likely that they were so startled to find him alive that they turned and ran down the beach toward the family shack to fetch their father.

The elder George Albright was not considered to be a very smart man. He lacked imagination, but was practical and possessed a common sense that prevented him from taking the wild stories of young boys too seriously. When his excited children ran to him babbling about a legless man washed up on the beach, George Sr. paid little attention.

The only reason a man would wash up on the beach was if there had been a shipwreck in the night, or if the poor soul was swept overboard in bad weather. It was not uncommon for shipwreck victims to appear on the shores of Digby Neck. Mr. Albright had noticed two unidentified schooners cruising offshore the night before, but they had disappeared by morning. While it had been raining overnight, there was no reason to believe the two anonymous ships had encountered any trouble. Besides, if there had been a wreck the night before, the fishermen of Sandy Cove would have been alerted and the entire village would have gathered on the beach in a rescue and salvage effort. Since no such commotion had occurred, George Sr. likely felt his boys were just getting into a bit of mischief with their story. He probably scolded the children and swatted at them before returning to his morning's work.

Unable to convince their father of their incredible discovery, the Albright boys went in search of some other adult. Collie took off toward the fields overlooking the ocean in hopes of finding a local farmer, while William went to locate his elderly grandmother.

Old Grandma Albright probably had little patience for her anxious grandson and his wild tale of a stranger on the beach. Fed up with being pestered by the boy, she finally relented and hobbled down to the beach to check out the story herself. The elderly woman was alarmed when she spotted the castaway. She returned to the Albright shack with all the speed she could muster to inform the boys' father that his children were indeed telling the truth about the legless man.

Meanwhile, Collie had found two local farmers working nearby. Robert Bishop, a young man of twenty-three, and his friend, William Eldridge, were busy tending their fields when they spotted the Albright boy running towards them.

The folks of Sandy Cove thought little of the Albrights and young Collie was considered somewhat simple-minded. After running up the hill from the beach the youngster was breathless, and he struggled to make himself understood. Bishop and Eldridge would have had trouble understanding the excited Collie, and it took some time before they figured out what all the commotion was about. After a few moments the farmers deciphered his ramblings and abandoned their work to follow the boy back to the shore. Given the garbled description of the scene that they heard from Collie, the farmers probably expected to find a dead body washed up on the sand.

What they saw when they reached the rock at the high-water mark must have stunned them. A pale, wasted young man, maybe in his late teens or early twenties, was struggling upon the sand. Both of his legs had been amputated above the knees.

He was clearly not dead. The stranger's eyes were wide with fear as he recoiled at the approach of the farmers. He thrashed about and began clawing at the sand, dragging his stiff, damp, cold body toward the water. He was trying to escape.

The stranger pulled himself into a sitting position. Then he lunged seaward by hoisting himself up on his hands and thrusting his torso forward, landing on his bottom. He moved forward by repeating this swinging manoeuvre over and over.

Propelling himself forward in this manner must have been extremely difficult. A double-amputee could master such a move over time, but only with a little practice after his wounds healed. Later, writers claimed that the sand was stained with blood from the castaway's freshly amputated legs, or that blood was seeping from the carefully bandaged stumps. But his actions on the sand that day indicate that his wounds were not as fresh as has been reported in later years.

Bishop and Eldridge could only guess that the unfortunate soul, overcome with grief and desperation, was heading to the ocean to drown himself. Annapolis judge and historian Alfred William Savary wrote dramatically about the castaway's supposed suicide attempt many years later in a personal letter. According to Savary, if the poor, abandoned stranger had succeeded in getting to the water: "He would have gone where thousands of his class, the waifs and strays of the lower grades of humanity from the great proletariat of our larger cities go every day, into oblivion, unknown and unwept, an infinitesimal drop in the vast ocean of human misery, suffering and death."

It is more likely that the strange castaway had developed a healthy mistrust of strangers by this time. The stranger was probably unconscious when first discovered by the Albright boys. When they poked him with a stick to see if he was indeed a corpse, they startled the groggy castaway. When the stranger heard Bishop, Eldridge, and Collie making their way back through the brush and toward him on the sand, his first instinct was to flee.

Taking the path of least resistance, the legless stranger attempted to escape by swinging his body downhill, toward the water. Despite his weakened condition, he still possessed remarkable strength. If he was actually trying to reach the water, he could certainly have used his strong arms to swim away from the three young men rushing toward the beach.

After Bishop and Eldridge recovered their senses from the astonishing scene before them, they hurried toward the stranger to hold him back and prevent him from plunging into the sea. He angrily resisted and fought back, but the able-bodied farmers managed to drag the castaway up the beach to safety.

Despite his vigorous thrashing, the man seemed to be in a state of shock. He was coughing violently and was soaked to the skin from the rain that had fallen before dawn. It was thought that perhaps the cold was causing his confusion, or that his sorry state was the result of the terror of his ordeal, or that maybe he had been drugged. His health seemed so poor it was believed that a few more hours of exposure would have killed him.

Soon George Albright Sr. joined the farmers on the beach near the rock. He had finally been persuaded by his son and elderly mother to go investigate the puzzling scene. Since the Albrights' house was the nearest shelter, the men decided to drag the stranger to the shack at the edge of the beach.

Near the rock where the stranger lay, the men found a small flask or jug of water and a tin box. Inside the box they discovered a chunk or two of black bread, known as hardtack or ship's biscuits. Whoever left the legless man on the beach in the night at least had the mercy to supply him with a few morsels of food and a mouthful of water.

Young Collie stood by while the adults rushed about fetching blankets to warm the shivering castaway, badgering him with questions all the while. It likely was not until many years had passed and amateur sleuths had quizzed Collie about his role in the discovery of the legless stranger that the Hermit even understood that the man he found on the sand that day had become a celebrity. Years later, many researchers and journalists who reported on the mysterious man tried to write Collie out of the story and give the credit of his discovery to other people. Perhaps it was thought that it would be more appropriate for Eldridge and Bishop, well-spoken and respected men of the community, to hold such an important role in the story—rather than the odd young boy.

The simple child could scarcely have predicted that his accidental discovery of a mysterious man on the beach would begin the first chapter of the saga of the man who would become known as Jerome—one of the most beloved legends in Nova Scotia. The tale that began on the remote beach that day spread from Sandy Cove to capture headlines around the world.

Chapter 2

The Unfortunate

The Albrights' small, rundown sea shack had never seen such commotion as it did that September day in 1863.

Collie Albright's mother, Catherine, was likely already boiling water for tea and preparing dry blankets by the time her husband burst through the door followed by the respected gentlemen, Eldridge and Bishop, who were carrying the legless half-corpse. Despite his earlier frantic attempt to propel himself down the beach, the unfortunate stranger had succumbed to cold and fatigue. He soon lost consciousness and the men who had carried him to the shack feared that death would quickly follow. If Collie and his brother had not discovered him when they did, he would be dead for sure.

They tried to warm the shivering castaway as best they could and quickly stripped off his soaked clothing. His garments were hung to dry as the gentlemen debated who should run to the village down the road to fetch medical help. Their primary concern was the rapidly declining health of the injured man whose terrible cough was getting worse.

Before long, word of the remarkable discovery on the beach on the Bay of Fundy side of Digby Neck spread among the people of Sandy Cove. As the day progressed, a parade of curious villagers descended upon the small cabin for a peek. The brief moments when the stranger drifted into consciousness were interrupted with questions from the villagers: What is your name? What is the name of your ship? Where are you from? What happened to your legs? They received no response, at least none they could decipher.

The Albright family would not have appreciated all the attention they received from the people of Sandy Cove as a result of their guest. Up until that point, the more affluent villagers had made it a habit to avoid the cabin by the beach and had largely ignored the odd, poor family. But over the following days, their cabin became a popular spot for locals to gather to gawk at the legless man and prod him with questions.

The Albrights looked after the legless stranger as best they could. For a poor fisherman like George Albright, it would have been a struggle to feed and clothe his own family, even with the help of his sons, let alone be responsible for the unfortunate wreck of a man who washed up on the beach near their cabin.

The castaway was not a gracious or agreeable house guest, either. Because he was near death when first discovered, it took a considerable amount of effort to nurse him back to some degree of health. He seemed angry and gloomy—no surprise considering his ordeal—but also refused to express any thanks or appreciation to his hosts and visitors for their efforts to make him more comfortable.

After asking the stranger countless questions in the days following his discovery, the villagers came to believe the man did not speak English, as his mumblings were thought to be in some unknown foreign language. The more educated members of the community tried to communicate with the confused castaway in as many languages as possible—French, Italian, Spanish, even Latin. At times it appeared he was struggling to make himself understood, but he would often give up in frustration.

One person who met the stranger during those first few days was the venerable Reverend J. C. Morse. Morse was a robust religious leader who commanded great respect in Sandy Cove. For sixty-two years he was responsible for the pastoral oversight of all the Baptist churches on Digby Neck. By the time of his death in 1907, Reverend Morse was one of the oldest clergymen in the province at eighty-eight years of age. He had performed the marriages of the majority of Sandy Cove's residents, baptized a good deal more, and probably buried the rest. It is unlikely that the community made any decisions regarding the decrepit castaway without first consulting Reverend Morse.

Like the other villagers, the learned Reverend Morse was not able to coax any useful information from the man during his initial visits. Ten days after the stranger was discovered, Reverend Morse was visited by an old friend from Bridgetown, Nova Scotia, named George Armstrong. Armstrong was a justice of the peace, and like the good reverend, a devout Christian. He was also an amateur geologist who had travelled to Digby Neck on that late summer day to do some rockhounding along the shores.

Reverend Morse, an eloquent and dramatic speaker, had probably regaled his old friend with the tale of the discovery of the legless castaway over a week earlier. With his curiosity appropriately aroused, Armstrong convinced Reverend Morse to guide him to the Albright home to view the silent stranger.

On September 18, 1863, Reverend Morse and George Armstrong set off on foot up the road from the village toward the Albright home. As they neared the cabin they found the unfortunate stranger sitting in the doorway, cautiously watching their approach. His physical condition had much improved, and the terrible cough he had suffered from a week earlier was starting to fade. By the time Armstrong came face to face with the stranger, the unfortunate had emerged from the crazed stupor that had gripped him following his discovery.

The first thing the visitors noticed was the bare stumps of the stranger's amputated legs. He was likely wearing breeches with the lower part of what remained of his legs exposed. "They were perfectly healed," wrote George Armstrong in a letter to the *Christian Messenger* newspaper on September 28, 1863. "The amputation seemed to have been done skillfully."

George Armstrong's letter was the very first written eyewitness account of the legless stranger, and provides an accurate picture of the man and the events surrounding his rescue. Armstrong had no reason to exaggerate what he saw. It is clear from his statement that the stranger's legs had not been recently amputated. This contradicts the many writers who, over the last century, have reported that the leg wounds were obviously new when he was discovered on the beach.

The late Yarmouth historian Arthur Thurston, who was a Civil War scholar, bought into the false idea that the castaway's legs appeared newly amputated. But Thurston did not believe that the blood that reportedly seeped from the stumps proved the injuries were fresh. In his historical column in the January 19, 1977, issue of the *Yarmouth Vanguard*, Thurston said, "the wounds of his double amputation seemed fresh to the layman. But it might take several years for such serious injuries to heal. Men wounded in battle in the 1860[s] still had unhealed hurts in the 1920[s]." Even a consummate historian like Thurston can get it wrong, as

George Armstrong's eyewitness account definitively answers the question of the condition of the castaway's legs immediately following his discovery.

While Armstrong proved to be a keen observer of the state of the man's legs, he did not describe other aspects of his physical appearance. Based on the castaway's dark complexion—after the colour returned to his face—other visitors to the Albright cabin believed he was Portuguese, Italian, or possibly Spanish. Robert Bishop, the gentleman farmer who helped rescue him from the beach, had spent some time in South America, and was familiar with the characteristics of people of Portuguese and Spanish descent. Bishop believed the stranger looked Portuguese rather than Spanish or Italian.

In the years to follow, the stranger's appearance when he was first discovered caused much speculation. Depictions of him in the newspapers ranged from swarthy to fair. In November 1898 a story in the *Halifax Herald* described the man when found as "apparently about 19 years old, with soft flaxen hair and blue eyes." Though a description in the April 20, 1912, edition of the *Halifax Chronicle* also said that he appeared to be about nineteen or twenty years of age, it stated that he was "dark complexioned." And a reporter from the *New York Herald* who met the legless man over forty years after he was discovered wrote on Sunday, December 9, 1906, that he had "no decisive racial characteristics. He might be an American… [however] the skin had formerly been very dark, in which case he easily could be pictured as an Italian or Spaniard."

Though Armstrong makes no mention of skin colour in his letter, he does support the idea that the man on the beach was European. Armstrong's letter indicates that the stranger was not as silent as later legends would have us believe, stating: "From certain words we got him to utter, I judged him to be a native of Spain, or perhaps Italy."

George Albright was home during Reverend Morse and Armstrong's visit, and he told the pair that his house guest seemed "more disposed to observe and communicate or try, than he had been since found." Instead of refusing to speak, there seemed to be some unknown reason why the man could not make himself understood. Apparently at some point during their meeting, the stranger repeated the word "*sise*" in answer to the visitor's questions, which Armstrong took to mean "yes."

In his letter to the *Christian Messenger* Armstrong revealed for the first time that the stranger was originally called Matteo or Matthew, writing "for such I think he wished us to understand his name." Armstrong did not say if it was he who determined that the stranger's name was Matteo, or if the villagers of Sandy Cove had given him this name. This is the only known reference to the name Matteo or Matthew, so it can be assumed he was not called by this name for very long.

Taking advantage of the afternoon, George Armstrong left Matteo and the Albright cottage to do some beachcombing along

Sandy Cove to search for curious rocks and geological specimens. As he walked along the shore it is doubtful his thoughts strayed too far from the desperate man he had seen sitting in the doorway. Before leaving the area at the end of the day, Armstrong decided to pay one last visit to Matteo to try to provoke him into talking. As he approached the cottage for a second time, Armstrong was struck with an idea. Perhaps if the name of his home country was mentioned, Matteo would react.

"*Hispania*! *Hispania*!" called out Armstrong. Remarkably, Matteo's face lit up with pleasure and recognition. He then bowed his head and uttered the word "*sise.*" Then Armstrong said, "*Italia*! *Italia*!" In reply, Matteo shook his head and answered, "*Non.*"

If the man called Matteo did indeed understand what was being spoken to him, then it seems obvious from his response that he was originally from Spain, rather than Italy. But could his responses have been misunderstood? Did Matteo really understand what was being asked of him? Or is it possible the stranger was being deliberately misleading—especially since it was felt by many that he was concealing some terrible secret?

Chapter 3

The Rumours

The villagers who crowded around the Albrights' doorway peered into the smoky cabin and speculated endlessly on the origins of the castaway. Interest in the stranger quickly grew beyond the borders of Sandy Cove, and tales about the man soon travelled up and down Digby Neck and across the bay to the French Shore.

When the villagers failed to get the castaway to answer their questions, they looked for other clues to his identity and origins. They could only imagine the circumstances that led to the abandonment of the man on the beach. The villagers of Sandy Cove were convinced that if only they could discover the name of the ship that discarded the legless man, the mystery would be easily solved.

The village residents remembered that an anonymous ship was seen offshore on the night before the stranger was discovered on their beach. Some even claimed that not only had one ship been spotted, but two. Bishop and Eldridge, the farmers who carried the castaway off the beach with young Collie Albright, later recalled watching at least one unidentified ship the day before. It hovered off the coast of Sandy Cove and seemed to drift back and forth until the blackness of nightfall devoured it. In the morning the mysterious ship was gone. Before it faded into the darkness, some witnesses claimed they spied movement on board as unknown sailors lowered a large bundle into a skiff and started rowing for shore.

At the time the ship, or ships, hadn't attracted much attention. It was not unusual to see foreign vessels cruising the waters off Digby Neck, since the Bay of Fundy had always been a busy waterway for shipping and fishing. Besides, there was a freshwater stream that emptied into the bay near the Sandy Cove beach, and the small skiff spotted disembarking from the ship may have been deployed to replenish the water supplies of the mysterious vessel.

As some witnesses recalled, the anonymous ships were pinkies—the pink-sterned schooners used to transport fish, lumber, and other cargo. Others disputed this, arguing that surely the exotic stranger had not been abandoned by a boat as common as a schooner.

If the anonymous ship could be identified, tracing it through the shipping registers of the nearest large ports—like Halifax and Yarmouth—and then tracking it down at its next destination would be a simple task. Using the name of the ship, the captain and crew could be found and brought to justice for the inhuman act they had committed. George Armstrong expressed his feelings on the matter, along with his staunch personal Christian leanings, in the letter he wrote to the *Christian Messenger* after visiting the stranger at the Albrights' home:

> What barbarity, inhumanity, cruelty and injustice does this act show in the perpetrators! Had the fear of God left their souls? Or love to man been expelled from their hearts? We hope the parties guilty of so mean and cowardly, so vile and wicked an act may be discovered, and made to feel the wrong they have done to this man, to Nova Scotia, to humanity, and to Christ.

Unfortunately, the ship, like the fog that shrouds St. Mary's Bay, remained elusive. Memory is a strange thing, and the collective memory of a small village in the grips of a fascinating mystery can evolve in unlikely ways.

The villagers considered the possibility that the ship was the naval vessel of a foreign nation. Due to the unusual nature of the castaway's injuries, and because he had been abandoned by a ship, it was thought that the man may have been a sailor whose legs were torn away by a well-aimed cannonball, or perhaps crushed under a mast that crashed to the deck in the midst of battle.

The most common way to lose a limb or two in the middle of the nineteenth century was, of course, on the battlefield, and it was guessed that the wretched man might have been a soldier mutilated in war. In 1863, the United States was divided by the bloody American Civil War. The worst riots in American history erupted in that year on the streets of New York after a desperate President Lincoln ordered the draft act, which forced unwilling men into military service. Some believed that the castaway was a wounded military officer exiled on the shores of Nova Scotia as punishment for desertion or another more shocking crime, like murder or treason.

It is possible the man was injured in the American Civil War, but there were still other battles raging even further south in the Americas. The man abandoned on the beach may have been a soldier in the famed French Foreign Legion, which was busy fighting for, and losing, French control in Mexico in the 1860s. In 1863, the same year the castaway appeared in Digby, a handful of French Foreign Legion troops were besieged by a much larger Mexican force at Camerone Hacienda, and supposedly fought to the last man. Since they were capable of such uncompromising bravery, the French Foreign Legion did not look with favour upon any hint of cowardice, surrender, or desertion among its troops. Punishment for insubordination in the French Foreign Legion was as unique as it is legendary. A disorderly legionnaire could expect to be forced to dig a narrow shaft in the sand and to stand in it unsheltered for days at a time. It would be safer for a legionnaire lacking courage to flee to the peaceful shores of Nova Scotia than to face the wrath of his officers or fellow soldiers.

There are those who felt the mysterious, tight-lipped stranger was not a simple foot soldier, but may have been a more glamorous spy. There were plenty of European spies afoot looking to exploit any new developments in the American Civil War. If his espionage were discovered, he may have been abandoned in Nova Scotia after his legs were removed as a stern warning that foreign spies would not be tolerated in the United States.

Speculation among the villagers about the stranger's origins was also fuelled by other clues that arrived on the shore with the castaway. When the men of Sandy Cove dragged the legless man from the seashore that damp morning, their primary concern was to get the stranger warm and dry, and to minimize the shock from which he appeared to be suffering. His wet clothes were stripped off and the shivering man set before a warm fire. At the time, no one took much notice of his dripping clothes hanging on a peg in the Albright cottage, but the clothing worn by the stranger soon became a source of much interest.

As the old chestnut goes, the clothes make the man—and in this story the clothes make the mystery. There are several different accounts of what the stranger was wearing on the day he was found. According to one version of the story, he was dressed in expensive European-style clothing, with a lined waistcoat and a finely knit shirt. Another popular version of the story contends that the castaway was found wearing a blue serge naval uniform. In the 1860s, blue serge was most closely associated with officers of the British navy; however, for hundreds of years, naval blue had been a popular uniform colour for fleets around the world. Even the regular crewmen of various navies wore blue shirts. It is very difficult to try to guess which navy, if any, the castaway could have been a member of based on rumours that he was wearing a blue uniform on the day he was discovered.

This tale becomes even more mysterious when the claim that all of the buttons, badges, and other military decoration had been carefully removed from the stranger's uniform is considered. With all manner of gold braid, brass buttons, badges, knots, and epaulettes adorning his uniform, an officer's jacket could be downright gaudy. In this era, a blank naval officer's uniform would have been an oddity indeed; however, there is no proof that the stranger's garments had any such decorations to begin with.

The truth is, despite the tales of the mysterious castaway's fine garments, there are no reliable first-hand accounts of what he was wearing when he was discovered. According to George Armstrong the castaway was left on the beach with some bread and "a small bundle of clothes." The stranger may have been left with an extra shirt or trousers for warmth, but Armstrong is silent on what this bundle of clothes looked like or what style of clothing he had on when he was found.

In addition to examining his clothes, the villagers carefully studied the castaway's body to see what stories his mannerisms and physical characteristics could tell. They looked closely at his young face and hands, and were puzzled to see that his fingers were quite delicate and soft. His hands seemed to betray a life of leisure. If the stranger had been a soldier or a sailor, as his injuries and clothing seemed to indicate, surely his hands would have displayed the same rough callouses and scars that marked the hands of the rugged fishermen and farmers of Sandy Cove.

In his letter to the *Christian Messenger*, George Armstrong wrote: "The man does not look warlike, nothing about him indicates war experience, except the loss of his legs." Historian Arthur Thurston agreed, writing in the *Yarmouth Vanguard* that because of the stranger's "lack of work-worn hands he was thought to be a gentleman."

They also examined the stranger's head for more clues to his background. At the time the practice of phrenology, the study of the shape and form of an individual's skull to determine characteristics such as intelligence and personality, was considered a legitimate science. The poor castaway was subjected to having his skull fondled and contemplated by those anxious to determine if he exhibited the head bumps that would indicate he was a nobleman. If his head didn't have the right bumps in the right spots, then he would be labelled an idiot. Luckily for him, more than one amateur phrenologist declared that he had a "well-shaped head," which suggested he was intelligent. This observation lent weight to the theory that he was a gentleman, and perhaps even royalty.

If the stranger were a gentleman of noble birth rather than a soldier, how did he come to be deposited on this remote beach in Nova Scotia? Soon a tale was spun about how the stranger was an exiled member of a royal family who was purposely mutilated and left for dead to clear the way for a pretender to the throne. The people of Digby Neck held a deep affection for royalty, as they were descendents of the Loyalists, who had remained loyal to the British Crown and fled the traitorous United States at the time of the American Revolution.

During the Victorian era it was quite fashionable for a country to boast of its very own mystery man, or woman, and it was preferable if there was a possibility that the mystery person du jour was a long-lost member of a royal family. The desire to believe that an anonymous vagabond could be royalty was overwhelming, and such a person brought attention and prestige to whatever town he or she wandered into.

If the story of an anonymous man believed to be of noble birth, banished into exile and forbidden to speak, sounds like it's been lifted from the pages of a romantic novel—indeed it has. As fantastic as this theory was, the possibility would not have seemed altogether impossible to the educated citizens of Digby Neck. Some of them would have been familiar with *The Man in the Iron Mask*, a novel written by Alexandre Dumas and published in 1848, just fifteen years before the stranger washed up in Sandy Cove.

Dumas based his work on popular legends and the writings of the revolutionary philosopher Voltaire, who was imprisoned in the Bastille in 1717. While in this Paris prison, Voltaire learned of a mysterious prisoner there many years before who was forced to wear a black velvet mask and was ordered to speak to no one. The guards said the prisoner was treated well on the orders of King Louis XIV, and lived in relatively luxurious cells.

The imaginative Voltaire concocted a theory that the masked prisoner was none other than the older brother of King Louis XIV, and the rightful heir to the throne. Alexandre Dumas wove even more intrigue and drama into the tale, making the anonymous prisoner the evil king's twin brother and replacing his velvet hood with a grim iron mask.

While these stories have been dismissed as fanciful by scholars, the truth behind the mystery of the silent masked prisoner has never been revealed. What is certain is that the man possessed a secret so sensitive to the ruling class of France that it was necessary to imprison him; yet he was valued, or adored, enough to make it unacceptable to simply execute him to guarantee his silence. He must have been easily identifiable, making it essential to conceal his face and stash him away in a remote place where few would have the chance to recognize him.

It does not take a large leap of the imagination to see how the people of Sandy Cove could have drawn a parallel between this legend and the mysterious, tight-lipped stranger who washed up on their shore.

While the story of *The Man in the Iron Mask* is not necessarily factual, subjecting a European royal to a similar indignity was not unheard of. Practically every influential European family is haunted by the treacherous plots of unsavoury ancestors. Such plots have involved poison, bombs, pretenders, usurpers, and even, literally, the odd stab in the back.

It has been said that the infamous foundling Kaspar Hauser was the victim of such a plot. The similarities between Kaspar Hauser and the stranger on Digby Neck are remarkable. Hauser stumbled into history in 1828 when he was found wandering the streets of Nuremburg, Germany. The teenager could barely speak, sputtering only a few words. Like the man who became known as Jerome, Kaspar caused quite a sensation, but unlike the castaway, Hauser seemed to enjoy the attention of all the visitors who came to ply him with questions. Speculation swirled around the youth and some felt he resembled Karl, the former grand duke of Baden. Conspiracy theorists whispered he was Karl's son and heir who was snatched as a baby by agents of Karl's uncle, Ludwig, a man who wanted power for himself. Hauser was murdered in 1833 by an unknown attacker.

He became a worldwide celebrity primarily because of the mystery of his origins and his inability to communicate exactly who he was or where he came from, much like the legless castaway discovered on the Sandy Cove beach in 1863.

With fantastic speculation being something of a hobby for many at the time, it would not have been unlikely for the legless man's caretakers to believe, or at least hope, that he was an exiled prince. But if so, what European royal house could the mysterious castaway claim as his birthright?

In 1863, Queen Victoria was soberly and firmly in charge of her empire. However, about thirty years earlier, her uncle, King George IV, scandalized the kingdom as a gluttonous rogue with a notorious reputation as a womanizer. King George IV reportedly fathered a number of illegitimate children, each with the potential to cause embarrassment to the throne. In order to save the monarchy from further scandal, the bastard offspring of the king were shipped off as quickly as they were born. Legend has it at least one son of the King of England was deposited in northern Nova Scotia, and became known as the Prince of Pictou. The lonely soul was a popular character in local taverns and celebrated in song by Nova Scotia singer-songwriter Dave Gunning on his album *Two-Bit World*. Since the man who was found at Sandy Cove beach was thought to be in his early twenties when he was discovered in 1863, it is doubtful he was related to King George IV who died in 1830; however, the legend of the Prince of Pictou proves many were willing to believe that Nova Scotia was not an entirely unlikely destination for exiled royalty.

At the time, there were other European royal families with countless skeletons shoved into every possible closet. The predominant dynasty in Europe during this period belonged to the Habsburgs, a family with a long, rich, and controversial history. Many of Digby Neck's residents believed that their mysterious castaway was Italian; while the seat of the Habsburg dynasty was the dual monarchy of Austria-Hungary, the family had a controlling interest in the fractured states of Italy. If the silent, legless stranger was an exiled member of some European royal family, and if he was from Italy, then he must have been a Habsburg. The Habsburgs were somehow involved in just about every possible political intrigue and conspiracy on the continent. Their position as the principal power brokers in Europe also made the family a target for ambitious power seekers and sordid blackmailers.

The Habsburgs were considered an occupying force in Italy, and were despised by those looking to unite the Italian states under Italian control. If the legless castaway were related to the Habsburgs in Italy at this time, he would have been entangled in the many political intrigues and plots underway to oust the Austrian rulers. Kidnappings, coercion, threats, and intimidation were all considered fair game during this time of political chaos.

It is also possible that the stranger was not a Habsburg prince, but a revolutionary who found himself on the losing side of an armed uprising and was forced to flee. Secret resistance groups were formed to undermine Habsburg control, the most infamous of which was the Carbonaria. The Carbonaria were modelled after the Freemasons, a secret society that demanded a vow of silence from each of its members. The failure of the Carbonaria to overthrow the Habsburgs left its members open to persecution, arrest, and even exile by the ruling Habsburg authorities. If Digby Neck's mystery man had been a member of the Carbonaria, he may have fled or been banished after being injured in a failed uprising. Perhaps an accident happened during his escape and he lost his legs. Forced to remain in exile while his countrymen fought for a unified Italy, the young man burned with silent fury and resentment.

Yet another theory was that he lost control of his temper one day and committed murder. In the uncontrolled outburst that resulted in him killing a man, he may have sustained terrible injuries to his legs. To avoid punishment, he fled across the Atlantic, vowing to never speak of his crime. He was a man on the run and in Nova Scotia he found a place where he could stop running.

One popular theory in the early twentieth century was that the legless castaway was a member of a vicious pirate crew. In the days after he was discovered on the beach, some of the villagers suggested that the vessel spotted offshore the night before he appeared might have been a pirate ship. The belief that he was betrayed by pirates was also supported by the stranger's supposed fury whenever the word pirate, or *forban* in French, was mentioned in his presence. Although the stereotypical swashbuckling buccaneer had pretty much faded away by the mid-1700s, the legalized or sanctioned piracy of American ships by British privateers continued well after the War of 1812. It is possible that pirates, in the guise of legitimate privateers, were still patrolling the sea lanes off the Bay of Fundy.

Another reason people were eager and willing to associate the legless castaway with pirates was a famous excavation taking place in Nova Scotia at that time. In 1863, just up the south shore of the province, Oak Island treasure hunters were busy digging for pirate gold and people were keen for any additional evidence linking pirates to Nova Scotia. New discoveries, such as links of gold chain and an artificial beach, gave treasure hunters hope that they were getting close to a major discovery. Exactly what lay buried on the island has always been a source of wild speculation—pirate gold, Shakespeare's lost manuscripts, and the jewels of Marie Antoinette are all possible contenders for the Oak Island treasure, according to a host of writers and explorers over the past two hundred years. But perhaps the most intriguing and controversial theory involves the most fabulous and elusive treasure of all time—the Holy Grail.

A popular and controversial theory among alternative historians contends that contrary to what is written in the Gospel, Jesus Christ married Mary Magdalene and the couple had children. The true purpose of the crusading warrior-monks known as the Knights Templar is said to be the protection of the Holy Grail, the vessel that held the blood of Christ—a symbolic description of a descendent who holds the blood of Jesus in his veins.

Anyone who knew this secret would be considered a dangerous enemy of the Vatican, since an actual descendent of Jesus himself could claim to trump the authority of a mere pope. Since the pope also reserved the duty to crown kings and emperors, a relative of Jesus could challenge the legitimacy of many of the ruling houses of Europe. According to supporters of the theory, the arrest and persecution of the Knights Templar in the 1300s, the Albigensian crusade, and the vicious crackdown on heresy known as the Inquisition were attempts by the Catholic Church to wipe out any memory of the children of Christ.

But the secret survived, and in some unusual places. In *Holy Grail Across the Atlantic: The Secret History of Canadian Discovery and Exploration* author Michael Bradley suggests that a written copy of the Jesus genealogies was smuggled from France to Scotland in the 1300s, and entrusted to members of Clan Sinclair. Some believe that in the 1390s Prince Henry Sinclair sailed to North America with the documents and stashed them in the most inaccessible and safest spot possible—the money pit at Oak Island, Nova Scotia. Bradley suggests the remains of a stone foundation in New Ross, a few kilometres inland from Oak Island, may be all that's left of a small fortress built by Sinclair as a refuge from which he could watch over and defend, if necessary, the treasure vault at Oak Island.

So what does this fantastic story have to do with the confused man abandoned and left for dead on Digby Neck? In a remarkable coincidence, the man who became known as Jerome wasn't the first to be marooned in this area. It happened once before on Long Island, the sea-bound extension of Digby Neck, over 260 years before the castaway washed up at Sandy Cove.

In 1604, the explorer Sieur de Monts sailed along the coast of what is now Nova Scotia, mapping the New World for the king of France. On board for this historic voyage was a young Catholic priest from a good Paris family named Nicholas Aubrey.

When de Monts anchored ship in St. Mary's Bay, a group went ashore on Long Island to explore and gather water. While on the island, Father Aubrey went missing. Though the crew fired the ship's cannon and blew trumpets for several days to help guide Aubrey through the forest, there was still no sign of the priest. Believing he was probably dead, the group set sail out of the bay, toward the present port of Annapolis.

When several of the explorers returned seventeen days later to investigate the possibility of silver and iron ore on the island, they were shocked to find Aubrey, furiously waving a handkerchief tied to a tree branch. Incredibly, though he lacked survival skills and would have been ill-equipped to cope in the forest, Aubrey had survived alone on Long Island.

Like the story of the castaway, the abandonment of Aubrey on Digby Neck leaves a number of unanswered questions. Author

Michael Bradley suggests that Aubrey did not go missing by accident. Digby Neck barely spans five kilometres at its widest point. It is unlikely that Aubrey could have wandered so far from the beach in such a short time that he was unable to hear the sound of cannonfire and trumpets coming from the ships in the bay.

According to Bradley, Father Nicholas Aubrey was a secret agent, initiated into the holy bloodline of Jesus Christ, who snuck away to deliver a message to the Knights Templar who still defended the Oak Island treasure vault from their fortress refuge at New Ross, Nova Scotia.

If this incredible story is to be believed, is it possible that Jerome was somehow also connected to the treasure supposedly buried at Oak Island—the secret of the Holy Grail of Jesus? It is a remarkable coincidence that not one, but two foreigners would find themselves abandoned by a ship under mysterious circumstances in nearly the same remote spot. As mentioned, when Jerome appeared on Digby Neck in 1863, there were a number of new discoveries happening on Oak Island, stirring up interest in the treasure hunt in newspapers around the world.

Many of the early explorers of Oak Island are known to have been associated with the Freemasons, who claim their fraternal order descends directly from the crusading Knights Templar. Some thought the castaway was a member of a secret society, and viewed his refusal to speak as an extreme example of the vow of secrecy members of groups such as the Masons must undertake.

Perhaps the castaway was stationed on Digby Neck as a silent sentinel, his legs amputated as a warning to anyone trying to find the treasure of the Holy Grail. Or his legs may have been chopped off as punishment for breaking the blood oath of his secret society and daring to seek the Oak Island treasure for himself.

Prince, pirate, soldier, spy—the theories surrounding the castaway's sudden appearance on Digby Neck are as varied as they are imaginative. But the legless man never encouraged any speculation about his origins. Unlike some later mystery men and women who made outrageous claims about their identities while participating in complicated money-making schemes, he never tried to convince people he was someone important. It wasn't what the stranger said that allowed observers to imagine a fantastic history for the silent man. It was what he didn't say. It was his silence that kept them guessing.

Chapter 4

The Gidneys

As rumours spread that the stranger was a wounded military officer, a noble-born European aristocrat, or maybe even royalty, it was likely deemed inappropriate for a gentleman of such stature to remain in the lower-class Albright home. The possibility that the castaway was a prince may even have created competition among the finer families of Digby Neck to host the seemingly noble stranger.

But who would have the ability, including the financial resources, to care for such a difficult house guest? More importantly, what family had the background, experience, and personal connections that could be best exploited to solve the mystery of this damaged stranger?

The community decided that the unfortunate castaway would be much better cared for in the home of William Gidney, a prosperous farmer who lived just up the road in the next village, Mink Cove. In an act of Christian charity or perhaps intense curiosity, Gidney graciously accepted this burden. The Gidney home was an appropriate place for the stranger to stay. After all, the community-minded family had a long history of involvement in the affairs of their fellow citizens. And William Gidney's brother Angus, a respected newspaperman, was an ideal resource to help track down the details needed to solve the puzzle of this marooned man.

Angus Morrison Gidney took over the management of the *Yarmouth Herald* in 1845. He used the pages of the *Yarmouth Herald* to vigorously promote his Christian values, especially his deep commitment to the temperance movement. Gidney's anti-drinking tirades made him a few enemies among the liquor-loving crowd in the port town of Yarmouth. In late 1850, he published an especially virulent anti-alcohol editorial. That night his newspaper office was trashed by burglars, who were likely drunk. They threw the type for the printing press down a well. Not long after, Angus Gidney left rowdy Yarmouth for the more civilized teetotalling villages of Digby Neck.

Upon arriving in Digby Neck, Angus sought out William. Just a year before, in 1849, William's wife, Priscilla, gave birth to a son who was given the traditional family name of Angus Morrison, just like his uncle. By the time he reached fourteen years of age, young Angus had been taught by his uncle and his father to take an active interest in politics, public service, and his community.

Just before his fourteenth birthday in November 1863 young Angus got his first glimpse of the legless stranger who had caused such a stir down the road in Sandy Cove. Later accounts described how the stranger loathed being moved from house to house, and his transfer to the Gidney home in Mink Cove likely did little to improve his bitter moodiness.

In the Gidney home, the castaway continued to be tight-lipped. There was no attempt, or even suggestion of trying to loosen the stranger's tongue with a nip of liquor since the Gidneys were zealous supporters of the temperance movement. The few words he did speak were difficult to decipher. Just as George Armstrong had attempted shortly after the stranger's rescue, the Gidneys probably tried to address the stranger with as many foreign language words as they could pronounce.

Despite mustering all their Christian charity, the Gidneys may have quickly become frustrated with their ungrateful new house guest. As the days dragged on and the stranger showed no eagerness to reveal his secrets, the burden of his care became less glamorous and desirable for the Gidney family and the people of Digby Neck. Despite the family's connections to knowledgeable and influential people across Nova Scotia, they were unable to gain any relevant clues as to where the castaway had come from and why he had been marooned on the Sandy Cove beach. William Gidney instead used his connections to try to find alternate living arrangements for this burdensome stranger.

If the man was Spanish, Portuguese, or Italian, he was almost certainly a Roman Catholic, and it probably seemed inappropriate for him to remain on the primarily Baptist Digby Neck, especially when there was a large Catholic community a short distance away across St. Mary's Bay. The absence of Roman Catholic households in Digby Neck was likely the primary reason the residents sent the stranger away from their community as soon as alternate lodging could be found.

Young Angus Gidney stood by and watched as his father made enquiries about which French Acadian family across the bay would be willing to take in the stranger. With help from a family friend named William Morton, William Gidney discovered that there was a man in the Acadian village of Meteghan who was from Europe and was known to speak several languages. Like almost everyone on the French Shore, this man, Jean Nicola, had a nickname—the Russian. Perhaps the well-travelled foreigner could be convinced to take over the care of the castaway, and maybe his ability to speak several languages would prove to be the key to communicating with the castaway. Nicola, perhaps eager to converse with another European who may have news from the continent, was enthusiastic about meeting and speaking with the legless mystery man.

William Morton handled the arrangements and soon plans were in place to ship the Gidney's house guest across St. Mary's Bay to Meteghan. The stranger was temporarily moved from the Gidney household in Mink Cove down the peninsula toward Digby, to Morton's home in Trout Cove (now known as Centreville).

The stranger remained tight-lipped while living with the Morton clan; however, on rare occasions he did display a sense of humour. During his time with the family the legless castaway amused himself by watching the children of the household. Many years later, Angus Gidney Boutlier (grandson of William's boy, Angus), recalled hearing stories of how the man enjoyed watching the children get into mischief: "[Mrs. Adelaide Morton] said he never spoke but if the kids got in devilry, he would laugh. He got a great kick out of the kids when they did something they shouldn't."

By the time the plans to send the silent man to live with the Russian in Meteghan were finalized, he had spent nearly five months living in Digby Neck. Young Angus Gidney may have been standing by, watching as the men of the village bundled the obstinate stranger onto a wagon and carted him away. The Gidneys must have felt a certain degree of regret over their inability to solve the mystery. But the removal of the legless castaway from Digby Neck did not end his association with the Gidneys. While they may never have seen each other again, Angus Gidney and his family were given another opportunity to try to solve the mystery many years later.

Chapter 5

The Russian

In February 1864, the legless mystery man was shipped to Meteghan. He likely travelled by boat, the quickest and easiest way to get to the other side of St. Mary's Bay. There would have been great excitement in the small village as the boat carrying the silent stranger slowly docked at the Meteghan wharf. The trip across the bay would not have been pleasant for the legless man; after all, the last time he had been on the water was the cold, rainy night when he was cruelly abandoned on an unfamiliar beach. He would have been in a foul mood by the time the little boat crossed the bay, and the throng of people on the wharf awaiting his arrival would have soured his spirits even more.

It was a short wagon ride up the road from the wharf to Jean "the Russian" Nicola's house. The villagers gathered around to stare at the strange legless man who was trying desperately to avoid their eyes and questions. At Nicola's house the crowd anxiously waited to hear what words, if any, he could compel from mystery man. They likely leaned forward as he asked, "What is your name?"

The stranger grunted a reply. Those within earshot were shocked to hear the silent man speak. He spat out a word—his name perhaps. He said something that sounded vaguely like "Jerome."

According to most written sources, the castaway was first called Jerome while on Digby Neck; however, there are conflicting reports as to when he first muttered this name. Forty-five years after he helped rescue the castaway on the beach, Robert Bishop claimed the man was heard to say something like Jerome when asked his name, but Bishop didn't say if he had heard this with his own ears.

Also looking back on his time with the mystery man forty-five years later, Angus Gidney said he never heard the man speak the word Jerome. Since the stranger stayed with the Gidney family, and he seemed more comfortable with young people, Angus would have been in the perfect position to hear him say his name, if he ever did. Acadian historian and author Edith Comeau-Tufts flatly refuses to believe the man was ever called Jerome while on Digby Neck. According to Comeau-Tufts it was not until the castaway was shipped across the bay to live among the Acadians in Meteghan that he gained the name Jerome.

Regardless of when he first uttered the word, does the name Jerome provide any clues to the man's mysterious past?

Jerome is not an uncommon name. But could it be possible that when the stranger uttered the word, he was not referring to his own name? If he were a Roman Catholic, as was believed, the man may have been praying to Saint Jerome. As he struggled to form words and make himself understood to the strangers confronting him in a foreign language, he may have called out to Saint Jerome, the patron saint of translators. Perhaps he believed Saint Jerome's divine intervention would help translate the confusing words being spoken at him.

Or perhaps the stranger was divulging his homeland, rather than his name when he spoke the word Jerome. The late Yarmouth historian Arthur Thurston speculated he might have been answering "Genova," in response to the question, "Where are you from?" Was the castaway trying to tell his benefactors he was from Genoa, the famous port city in northern Italy? The stranger's dark, swarthy complexion had led some witnesses to believe the man was Italian, so it was entirely possible he was Genoese.

While on Digby Neck people seemed to believe his name was Matteo, and in Clare he was known as Jerome. His actual name may sound like a cross between the two. Regardless of what he was trying to communicate when he muttered what sounded like Jerome, this was the name by which the mysterious stranger would become known around the world.

If the crowd that gathered around the Russian in Meteghan that day hoped to learn the mystery behind the stranger, they were disappointed. He refused to reveal any more information. It was believed the legless man was too stubborn and proud to respond to Nicola, who repeated his questions in different languages.

The truth is Nicola likely knew just enough of several languages to get by. He did not speak either French or Italian very well, despite later newspaper articles claiming he was fluent in these languages. He was an uneducated soldier from Corsica, a backward island country, with a thick accent. Respected historian, politician, and judge Alfred William Savary referred to Nicola as a "very rough and ignorant man with an impediment in his speech and not able to annunciate plainly in Italian, French or English," in a letter to the *Saint John Daily Telegraph* in April 1909. It is not surprising Nicola was unable to successfully communicate with Jerome. Even if Nicola, with his thick Corsican accent and broken French and Italian, could make Jerome understand the questions he asked, he may have lacked the skill to comprehend Jerome's replies.

George Armstrong, who wrote about Jerome only a few weeks after he was discovered at Sandy Cove, was convinced Jerome was from Spain after he got a response from the legless stranger when he addressed him in Spanish; however, Jean Nicola could not speak Spanish at all. If Jerome were indeed from Spain it would have been a waste of time for Nicola to interrogate the mysterious stranger who had just arrived on his doorstep.

Like Jerome himself, Nicola was quite a curiosity when he arrived in the tiny Acadian village. As a newcomer to Meteghan, Nova Scotia, Jean Nicola likely experienced the same feelings Jerome did when he arrived in the town a few years later. Nicola knew the uncertainty of being a stranger, the shame of being an outcast, and the fear of being a prisoner.

It is believed Nicola was born in the town of Ajaccio, Corsica. Growing up, Jean Nicola would have spoken Corse, a local dialect made up of a rough form of Italian and French.

Since Corsica had for many years been ruled by the city state of Genoa, many Corsicans felt a closer affinity to the Genoese than the French. This connection led Nicola to leave Corsica for the island of Sardinia in the 1850s, which was still under the control of Genoa. After abandoning his home in Corsica there were few opportunities except military service for Jean Nicola, a poorly educated peasant. Joining the army guaranteed steady pay, regular meals, and warm clothes.

In 1854, Jean Nicola found himself preparing for conflict, as the contingent from Sardinia joined France and Britain in aid of the Ottoman Empire in the Crimean War against the Russians (1853–1856). Many written accounts of the Jerome story mention the fact that Jean Nicola was a soldier who was taken prisoner during the Crimean War. It was often assumed he was captured in battle;

however, there is evidence to suggest Nicola was involved in something less heroic—something traitorous.

Just over one hundred years after the Crimean War, reporter Joe LeBlanc wrote in the *Halifax Chronicle-Herald* on December 13, 1954, about the popular rumour surrounding Jean Nicola's military secret: "The man, known as Nicholas, was said to have been a deserter from the Napoleon army." Napoleon's army refers to the French army under Napoleon III, as it was mistakenly assumed that Nicola, being a Corsican, was fighting for France instead of the Sardinian contingent.

Whether it happened in the midst of combat, or as a result of the traitorous actions of a deserter, Jean Nicola was most likely captured by the Russians during the Battle of the Tchernaya in August 1855.

While the life of a fighting soldier was wretched, the conditions for a prisoner of war, especially someone believed to be a deserter, were abominable. Prisoners were often infested with lice and fleas, and suffered from painful dysentery. As for deserters, they were distrusted by the Russians and treated like criminals rather than prisoners of war. Deserters also received regular beatings from their fellow captive countrymen, which were overlooked by their Russian guards.

Being robbed of his freedom would have been unbearable for a Corsican like Nicola. Nicola, along with twenty fellow prisoners, made a daring escape from his Russian captors.

Once he reached safety, Nicola likely had little enthusiasm for returning to the front lines of battle. If he were indeed a deserter he would have been subjected to severe punishment and imprisonment if he reported back to the military authorities. Sea captains from Yarmouth, Nova Scotia, regularly sailed shiploads of coal to the Black Sea to feed the war machine in the Crimea. Nicola likely gained passage aboard such a ship on its return voyage and soon found himself on the busy Yarmouth waterfront. From here he probably boarded a steamer to Meteghan.

Soldiers learning new languages often memorize the curse words first. During his time as a prisoner of war, Nicola would have picked up Russian expletives, and likely resorted to spewing these curses in moments of frustration. His use of this Slavic language, and his stories about his capture during the war, likely resulted in his new nickname—the Russian. In time, his ability to roughly converse in Italian would have endeared him to John Meechi, an Italian barber who set up shop in the village a few years later. Meechi, like Nicola, was a former soldier and the two could have swapped war stories about taking up arms for the Italians.

After settling in Meteghan, the Russian had to find ways to support himself. He likely hired out his strong back for odd jobs on the wharf, in the fields, and in the logging woods. He also made extra money by playing the organ in the area. With the money he made, Nicola was soon able to afford a small rundown house on the busy main road in Meteghan. The enterprising newcomer turned the shabby building into a boarding house and supplemented his meagre income by renting out rooms to strangers.

Nicola's next step to becoming a respectable member of the community was to find a wife. The gruff stranger caught the eye of a local widow named Julitte Comeau, who was eager to find a new husband to support her and her six-year-old daughter, Madeleine Genevieve. Jean Nicola married Julitte on January 23, 1857, and she and little Madeleine moved into his boarding house in Meteghan.

In 1864, when he was informed that Jerome needed a place to stay, the Russian realized that providing room and board for the castaway was a unique business opportunity, so Jean Nicola and Julitte agreed to care for the stranger. There seemed to be a great deal of interest in this mysterious man, and if the local authorities were willing to pay for his lodging Nicola would be guaranteed a modest, yet regular income. The enterprising Corsican soon arranged with local officials to have the tab for Jerome's rent and board picked up by the Nova Scotia Government.

Jerome's forced relocation from Digby Neck to Meteghan did not improve the gloomy, foul mood that had enveloped him since the day of his discovery, yet there were a few rare times when he did express brief periods of joy. Despite his frequent fits of frustration and anger, Jerome displayed sincere affection for Nicola's stepdaughter, Madeleine. The pair could be seen playing together in the fields. Madeleine was quoted as saying that Jerome "could walk very well after his legs healed," in the December 9, 1906, issue of the *New York Herald.* She added, "When we were together he would play with me and could run as fast as I could."

Jerome often entertained Madeleine and her young friends by performing feats of strength. Jerome would go to the woodpile and hold his arm out so the youngsters could stack wood upon it. According to Madeleine, they "could never put enough wood on his arm to make him take it down. Then he would walk into the house with the tremendous loads, holding his arm right out straight but always looking down."

Nicola may have been amused by the relationship between Jerome and Madeleine, but he was uncomfortable with the close bond that developed between his wife and their silent house guest. Caring for the legless man took a great deal of Julitte's time. It is possible the relationship between Jerome and Julitte caused Nicola to feel resentful. Nicola may have been jealous of Jerome, and not only because a loving connection was developing between his wife and a stranger, but because the people of Meteghan had shown Jerome a hospitality and kindness that was denied the Russian himself. While Nicola had worked hard to gain acceptance in the small community, Jerome was welcomed without question. The Russian had scraped together a living for himself and his family while others seemed willing to lavish gifts and attention on the seemingly ungrateful Jerome. The many people who were willing to believe Jerome was of European nobility, and maybe even royalty, treated him with respect and dignity while Nicola lived with the shame of being a military deserter from a poor family. By caring for the silent mystery man, Nicola may have hoped some of the adoration and fascination that was ignored by Jerome would be transferred to him. Perhaps it was jealousy-fuelled resentment that prompted Nicola to play a cruel joke on Jerome one evening.

Most nights after supper, Jerome would sit out on the porch alone or climb out an upper window onto the roof to look at the stars. Frustrated by his refusal to talk, Nicola came up with a scheme to frighten a response from Jerome. He gathered a bundle of sticks and fashioned them together to form the crude skeleton of a man. Nicola then tossed a clean white sheet over his stick man to create what must have resembled a stiff, awkward ghost. While Jerome was distracted, gazing at the stars in the night sky, Nicola quickly placed his ghostly creation on the porch nearby.

Jerome looked over at the manufactured ghost and quietly stared at it for a moment. He then hobbled inside the house. A minute or two later he returned to the porch to stare at the strange figure again. Annoyed by Jerome's lack of response to his creation, Nicola rushed up to him and shouted out, "Look Jerome, it is the devil!"

Jerome, unimpressed by the prank, finally spoke one of the few complete phrases he is ever known to have uttered. "The devil is not white," Jerome replied sullenly. He then turned around and crept back into the house. Julitte's daughter, Madeleine, later recalled that Jerome rarely ventured outside to look at the stars after that incident. Perhaps he was insulted by the trick Nicola played on him, or maybe he was more disturbed by it than he let on. Jerome was a man who grappled with his devils in silence, and he likely knew the colour of their skin very well.

It is unknown what Julitte thought of her husband's cruel joke. The sensible Acadian woman probably felt that playing such a trick on their house guest was not very funny. She may have tried to comfort Jerome after the experience, which would have fuelled her husband's jealousy further.

His muttering about the devil provides further evidence that Jerome had the ability to talk, despite the most popular versions of the legend that suggest he never spoke at all. Most of the words that Jerome is ever known to have spoken were uttered while he was living at the Russian's home. Over the five or so years Jerome lived in his house, Nicola was able to coax or trick Jerome into speaking a number of words and phrases; however, it was on an evening when Jerome was quiet, content, and seemingly enjoy-ing a rare moment of peace, that the Russian got an unexpected response to a tired question. When interviewed by an American newspaper reporter many years later, Madeleine Genevieve remembered that on that night, when her stepfather asked Jerome the name of the ship he had travelled on, "he answered right away it was the *Colombo.*" Madeleine recalled that any time Jerome spoke "he turned pale and showed great fear and would not speak anymore for a long time." After suddenly blurting out the word *Colombo,* she said he was especially agitated, and "turned ashy and trembled violently and showed much more fear even than before."

Jean Nicola would not only have been shocked that Jerome answered the question, but also to hear such a familiar word. According to Corsican legends, explorer Christopher Columbus himself was born on the island, and not in Genoa, Italy, as the history books say. The name Colombo derives from the same root as Columbus and is a common family name in Corsica. Jerome too is a common name in Corsica. When the legless castaway mumbled an answer to the question put to him, Jean Nicola would have been intrigued to hear words that reminded him of his homeland. Perhaps for a moment Nicola believed Jerome himself was a fellow Corsican from his homeland, but no amount of badgering could convince Jerome to reveal any more information.

If Jerome had arrived on a ship called *Colombo*, or some variation of that name, solving the mystery would be a simple matter of finding the vessel; however, tracing the voyages of all the ships named for Columbus in the mid-1800s is a nearly impossible task. Even today, with the available resources and databases of ships, and crew and passenger lists from this time period, the chances of finding the right ship are slim to none. Poring over the shipping news columns in old newspapers, leafing through books on maritime history, and conducting Internet searches of shipping lists has produced a large number of ships with names that sound like Colombo, several of which could have been involved in the

Jerome affair. The Maritime Studies Research Unit of Memorial University in St. John's, Newfoundland, produced a comprehensive CD entitled *Ships and Seafarers of Atlantic Canada*, which lists at least thirty-eight ships during this era with some form of Columbus as their name.

Bad luck seems to plague ships named for Columbus. Sailors and shipowners are a superstitious lot, so it seems odd that they continued to name ships after Christopher Columbus even though so much tragedy surrounded ships christened with this moniker. The *Columbia*, launched from Bremen, Germany, on October 17, 1846, was used to carry immigrants to New York twice a year and returned to Europe loaded with tobacco or cotton. Perhaps Jerome sailed to North America aboard this ship. In August 1879, the *Columbia* was headed to Quebec when the ship struck a whale and sank. Luckily the crew was rescued by a steamer.

Another ill-fated *Columbia* was also launched in 1846 in New York. Not long after this square-rigger was launched, it encountered a terrible winter gale while crossing the Atlantic. When the captain and some officers were swept away by a large wave, the remaining crew became frenzied. The crew terrorized the passengers and ransacked the cabins. The frightened passengers were saved when another vessel came alongside and armed sailors brought an end to the mutiny. Despite this tragic event early in its history, the *Columbia* went on to a long career on the ocean and was still sailing in 1887, making it possible that this was the vessel that transported Jerome.

A side-paddlewheeler named *Columbia* was launched on November 27, 1856, to be used for shipping between New York and Charleston. This ship later took up a cross-Atlantic run to Liverpool. Again, the dates for this ship and its use in transatlantic service indicate that it may have been Jerome's ship.

The theory that Jerome was a soldier is reinforced by the discovery of a ship named *Colombo* that was prominent during the Crimean War (1853–1856). This *Colombo* was an English steamer used for the crossing from Varna to the Calamita Bay landing, and for towing ammunition barges. It is not impossible Jerome served on this ship, and lost his legs during the Crimean War.

The 1861 barque *Columbus* was launched from Bremen and carried petroleum and passengers from the United States to Europe. Lloyd's Register for 1864–1865 cites a barque named *Colombo* built and registered in Sunderland, England, in 1863. Since Jerome was abandoned on Digby Neck in 1863, these ships should be possible culprits.

However, there remains the possibility that searching for the *Colombo* off the coast of Digby Neck in 1863 is a matter of looking for the wrong ship at the wrong time. Something that didn't seem to occur to the people who were speculating on how Jerome ended up on the beach at the time of his discovery, or to many early writers about the story, is that perhaps two ships were involved in Jerome's story. It is possible that one ship cruelly dumped Jerome on the beach in 1863, while an entirely different vessel—perhaps the

Colombo that Jerome mentioned—originally transported Jerome to North America. If so, the search for the Colombo connected to Jerome becomes much more difficult. Rather than simply searching for a Colombo that travelled to Nova Scotia in 1863, a much broader time frame must be taken into consideration.

Despite speculating endlessly about his ship, those who were concerned with solving the mystery of Jerome were getting nowhere. The clue he offered when he muttered the word Colombo was not enough to help reveal his identity. But he had a little more to say.

Jean Nicola also managed to catch his house guest off guard when he suddenly asked Jerome where he came from. Jerome replied simply, "Trieste."

Jean Nicola's acquaintance John Meechi, the Italian merchant and barber, had visited Jerome in Meteghan and declared that his accent and choice of words suggested that he was from northern Italy. Specifically, Jerome's dialect seemed to be from along the Adriatic Coast, where the port city of Trieste is located, suggesting that Jerome had provided a truthful answer to Nicola's question. At the time, the city of Trieste was occupied by the Austro-Hungarian Habsburg dynasty. Uttering what sounded like Trieste confirmed for many that Jerome was an exiled Habsburg prince.

However, Jerome's infrequent mutterings were hard to decipher at the best of times. The word Trieste closely resembles an old French word *tristesse*, meaning sad or melancholy. Perhaps he was not revealing the name of his hometown when Nicola thought he said Trieste, but was saying *tristesse* in an attempt to give some insight into his forlorn and fragile emotional state. When asked where he was from, maybe Jerome was trying to say he came from an unhappy place.

It seemed that Jerome was most likely to speak when he was quiet, content, and at peace. With his mind perhaps drifting, recalling happier times, Jerome seemed to forget himself, and forget he was unable or unwilling to talk. Witnesses said Jerome was happiest in the company of small children, like William Morton's kids and Madeleine, and could be seen speaking with youngsters when no adults were within earshot. Apparently he enjoyed teaching youngsters the names of different objects in foreign languages. Around adults he behaved very differently and was guarded and fearful.

His comfort and peaceful demeanour among children was in stark contrast to the distress he displayed after accidentally speaking in front of adults. After unconsciously, or carelessly uttering a word like Colombo or Trieste, Jerome was horrified. Why did Jerome display such fear after speaking? Many people believe that Jerome felt he had revealed too much. Jerome, like the man in the iron mask, may have been forbidden to speak. Perhaps his torturers cemented his silence by threatening to harm his loved ones, and his legs were chopped off to demonstrate how serious their evil intentions were. When he absent-mindedly said Colombo and Trieste, he may have inadvertently let slip a bit of secret information and feared the consequences. If he was under some solemn oath of secrecy, or if he had agreed to remain silent in a terrible plea bargain for his safety, the accidental uttering of these words could have cost him his life.

Perhaps Jerome was uneasy when speaking in front of the Russian because he did not feel entirely safe in the seeming comfort of the Meteghan boarding house. His reluctance to speak, even after it became apparent that he could, would certainly have angered the impatient Nicola.

It seems Jerome did not respect his host and acted out against the Russian. He would try to escape from the house and refused to obey the directions Jean Nicola gave him. In a conversation with writer J. Alphonse Deveau in 1971, a Meteghan local named Joe Sullivan recalled that Jerome was an *"etait un diable,"* or a little devil, who constantly agitated and infuriated Nicola. The tension between the two stubborn men grew until it exploded into violence. As a former soldier, Nicola knew of only one way to deal with insubordination. He whipped Jerome furiously. Witnesses remembered watching Jerome crawl out of the house onto the dirt road, followed by the Russian, who clutched his whip and beat the legless man in the street. The silence of Jerome in the face of such punishment likely fuelled Nicola's anger more, and his lashings became more ferocious.

Jerome was a powerful man. If the two were on an equal footing and the Russian had bullied his house guest, he would have had a battle on his hands. Jerome knew he could have defended himself against the whip if only he could have faced Nicola eye to eye. Jerome was also a proud man. Receiving the lashings from the Russian would have been more than just a painful torture. Physical pain is something Jerome had learned to endure in silence. The humiliation of being whipped by a brutish lout in front of Julitte and her daughter—two women he seemed to respect and adore—would leave far more damaging psychological scars upon Jerome.

When questioned about Jerome's sanity, Madeleine Genevieve recalled a horribly violent outburst directed against a house pet. She explained to a reporter from the *New York Herald* that sometimes Jerome "would have fits of rage…One night a cat jumped on his bed and he grabbed it and tore it right in two."

Killing a playful cat with his bare hands seems particularly cruel, even for the normally disgruntled Jerome. Perhaps this disturbing and seemingly inexplicable act of violence was provoked by the frustration he felt over the cruel treatment he received at the hands of the Russian.

Julitte passed away in 1865, possibly from tuberculosis. Her death had a significant impact on Jerome. The 1994 award-winning film *Le Secret de Jérôme*, explored the relationship between Julitte and Jerome in a highly fictitious way. It is doubtful that Julitte had a sexual relationship with Jerome, as was portrayed in the movie; however, Madeleine remembered that the pair were very close right up until the time of her mother's death: "[Jerome] seemed very fond of my mother. When she died, he went to her bed and examined her feet and toes, and when he was satisfied she was really dead the tears rolled down his cheeks and he took the cross in his arms and sat by her for a long time."

There are few accounts of Jerome speaking after Julitte's death. He had been abandoned by those he trusted before, but the death of Julitte caused him to withdraw even more completely. Jerome was now left alone with the Russian, a man who abused him physically and mentally, and Julitte was no longer there to protect him.

His silence deepened. The sombre mood of mourning that descended over the household and Jerome's growing introversion likely did not help the strained relationship between Jean Nicola and his boarder. Not long after Julitte died Jean Nicola married Victoire Comeau. The pair had a daughter who died in infancy. Even with a new wife the Russian had thoughts of returning to Corsica.

He would have been free to leave his family in Meteghan as his stepdaughter Madeleine Genevieve was a grown young woman and was probably married by this time to a gentleman named Doucet. As for Jerome, arrangements were made to send him down the road to live with the family of Victoire's brother, Dedier, who ran the postal stop in Cheticamp (now called Saint Alphonse). It was felt Jerome might find a good home there.

The Russian set sail for his homeland around the year 1870. Jean Nicola, the man known as the Russian, died while overseas and never saw Nova Scotia or Jerome again.

Chapter 6

The Saints

In the late 1800s, the people of the community of Saint Alphonse went about their daily business of farming, logging, and fishing, as travellers between Yarmouth and Digby passed by on the regular stagecoach. Most travellers chose to refresh themselves at the coach stop in nearby Meteghan. The few outsiders who stopped in Saint Alphonse did so only because the stagecoach was obligated to drop off and pick up mail in the community.

The postal stop in Saint Alphonse was the home of Dedier and Elizabeth "Zabeth" Comeau. If it had not served as the post office, few travellers would have noticed the unremarkable house located on the main coach road somewhere between Mardi Gras and Bear Cove roads. Built in the austere style of the humble Acadians, the home was likely constructed with wood cut and hewn by Dedier Comeau himself, with help from his male relatives and neighbours.

One day in the late 1860s, news came from up the road in Meteghan that their brother-in-law, Jean Nicola, was leaving the village to return to his native Corsica. That meant his famous house guest, the mystery man named Jerome, was in need of a place to stay. In failing health, Victoire may have appealed to her brother for help, leaving Dedier and his wife Zabeth to argue over the benefits and disadvantages of opening their home to the stranger.

By this time, Dedier and Zabeth had been married for several years. The spirited Zabeth was fourteen years younger than her husband when they married on November 11, 1862. His young bride brought a refreshing and robust energy to Dedier's home. Zabeth was described by author Edith Comeau-Tufts in her book *Acadienne de Clare* as "simple and humble. Short and stout with the air of a rolling ball…walking swiftly in her daily visits to the neighbours."

As expected, Dedier and Zabeth began producing children almost immediately. The young couple had five children at first and then eight more. Unfortunately, infant mortality was high in those days, and the Comeaus lost three children while still babies. There would be little time to mourn their deaths as Zabeth had other young children and a husband to care for.

With the demands of a growing family, it seems unlikely that Zabeth would have been enthusiastic about accepting a strange boarder into her home; however, the couple agreed to care for Jerome. While the Acadian people are honest folk, they are also industrious and entrepreneurial. Like Jean Nicola, Jerome's former caretaker, the Comeaus saw the legless man as not just a house guest, but a business opportunity. Jerome came with his own income, as the enterprising Russian had arranged for the Province of Nova Scotia to provide for his upkeep as a transient pauper to the tune of two dollars per week. The "Jerome item" was a regular line in the financial returns of the government's Blue Books, the annual provincial budget documents. According to the dossier in the Nova Scotia Archives, the government provided $104 each year initially, but the stipend allotted to care for Jerome grew over the years. While $104 annually was a modest sum, it provided an attractive incentive for a seasonal labourer with a growing family like Dedier.

Around 1870, a glum Jerome was once again loaded onto a wagon like so much luggage and carted down the dirt path to yet another home of strangers. Another forced relocation would have damaged even further whatever fragile trust Jerome allowed himself to share with the people of Clare. At least his new home had the two ingredients that seemed to bring some joy to Jerome—a warm stove and small children.

Jerome was genuinely fond of children. The few times he expressed joy or compassion, he was in the company of youngsters.

He allowed himself to share things with children he kept suspiciously guarded from adults. When questioned by children about his injuries or his origins, he appeared to mutter responses not meant for grown-ups to hear. It seems Jerome recognized that he shared many things in common with children. He was vulnerable, misunderstood, and dependent on others.

The children who played with Jerome recalled many years later that the legless man often spoke with them when adults were not around. As he had been at the Morton house, Jerome was especially amused when the Comeau children got into mischief. He sat and watched as the children caused trouble, breaking his silence with a peal of laughter as Zabeth scrambled to dish out punishment. "If I catch you I'll warm your backside," Zabeth would often holler, but the children knew this threat sounded more painful than the actual punishment would be.

For their part, the kids seemed to regard Jerome like a playful family pet. With his strong arms, Jerome would scoop small children up into his lap, patting them on their heads. As he curled up by the cookstove like a dog, the little ones would romp near Jerome, occasionally sharing sweets with him.

Jerome had a sweet tooth and though he gladly accepted candy from children, he angrily waved off gifts from adults. Observers who were inclined to believe Jerome was descended from European royalty may have regarded this refusal of gifts from adults as another sign of his nobility. In some countries it is customary for a monarch to only accept gifts from other monarchs.

It was during an exchange of sweets between Jerome and a child that one of the strangest, and most famous, events in his mysterious story occurred.

It was sometime in the early 1880s—after Jerome had lived with the Comeaus for about ten years—when the Blackadar company wagon pulled into the yard of the Comeau home as it had done so many times in the past. On that day, young George Day Blackadar carried a small package of dried fruit and candy that was manufactured at his family's store in Hectanooga. The village of Hectanooga was practically owned by the Blackadar family and was home to several of their sawmills. The family had established itself in the lumber industry in the backwoods of Digby County. As a youngster, George worked for Blackadar and Company, the family store, and would accompany his older relatives on deliveries along the French Shore of Clare. It would not have been uncommon for the Blackadar boys to visit the postal stop in Saint Alphonse during their delivery rounds.

Young George was likely fascinated by the strange foreigner with the missing lower limbs who huddled around the wood stove. Like other children who came to visit, George planned to hand over his candy treats to the odd spectacle named Jerome, and maybe tease the grumpy man a bit in an attempt to make him speak or at least growl like a dog, as he was known to do.

As the horses halted and the wagon rolled to a stop, young George saw two women he did not recognize emerge from the

Comeau house. As the local postal stop, the Comeau home was a popular place to visit, especially for those hoping to catch a glimpse of the legendary Jerome; however, the two women in the doorway on this day were different, if only because they obviously created excitement within the house. As they walked away, young George Blackadar overheard the women whispering to each other. One woman was heard saying, "He is well here. Let us leave him be."

George entered the house as the women were leaving and listened as the agitated Comeau family excitedly talked about what had just happened. Less than an hour earlier, the two anonymous women had appeared on the Comeau doorstep and asked if this was the home of the man with the missing legs. They did not divulge who they were, where they came from, or the reason for their visit. They were led into the kitchen where they approached Jerome, who regarded them suspiciously. The two women made it known they wanted to speak with Jerome in private. The legless man dragged himself to his room, followed by the strangers, and the door was shut behind them.

From behind the closed door, the hushed voices of the women could be heard. Then, to the utter amazement of the eavesdropping Comeau family, Jerome began to speak in response. The conversation between the three continued for some time, with Jerome taking an active part in the dialogue. According to the Comeaus, the trio did not speak French. Their whispers were in a language unfamiliar to the Comeaus. After all these years, Jerome was speaking quite clearly, but no one within earshot could understand a word.

After a time, the door opened. The women stepped out, thanked their hosts graciously, and left. The family was likely too shocked to question the women about their visit with Jerome. Or perhaps the women, in their manner or appearance, intimidated the Comeau family who felt it wise to allow them to leave unmolested.

The tale of the two anonymous women who mysteriously visited the Comeau home has long been a staple in the legend of Jerome. The story is just vague and mysterious enough to be easily dismissed as yet another tall tale that was added to the fantastic Jerome saga many years later—if not for the corroboration of Major George Day Blackadar, a reputable, trustworthy source. Blackadar, the young delivery boy who saw the women at the Comeau home that day, went on to become a member of Parliament, and was the longest-serving military cadet instructor in Canada when he retired in 1944. The revelation of Blackadar's role in the event is an unlikely piece of storytelling in itself.

On December 7, 1966, prolific writer and historian Robert Blauveldt (1894–1975) wrote about Jerome in the front-page article of a supplement to the *Yarmouth Vanguard* called "Jerome—The 'Mystery Man' of Clare." In the article, Blauveldt described twenty-five years of research into the Jerome story, and how he travelled to the district of Clare one day to personally interview people about the story of the two mysterious visitors. Amazingly, the enthusiastic and talented researcher could not track down anyone who could provide more information about the story.

Blauveldt returned to Yarmouth that night without discovering anything new about Jerome and the mysterious women. Upon his arrival in Yarmouth, Blauveldt happened upon his old friend, the retired teacher Major George Blackadar. When Blauveldt told the old major about his fruitless fact-finding mission to the French Shore, Blackadar surprised the writer by asking, "Did you ever hear about the women who came to see him?" Blackadar then confessed he had witnessed the odd event as a boy, and related the story of the two female visitors in detail.

Despite his coincidental good luck in confirming the story, Blauveldt was still unable to discover the purpose of the women's visit. To add even more credence to the story, writer J. Alphonse Deveau, who has written extensively about Jerome, verified Major Blackadar's story. Deveau's aunt married Charles Comeau, son of Zabeth and Dedier, and she had told her family the same tale.

There has been much speculation about the identity of the mysterious pair, and about why Jerome submitted himself so easily to their interrogation, when it was well known he despised any confrontation with strangers.

Although Jerome was difficult and contrary with men, like some chivalrous noble of old he often displayed a tenderness and gentleness toward certain women, particularly Julitte, Jean Nicola's first wife. A friend of the Comeaus said that after Jerome was established in the family's home in Saint Alphonse, Zabeth Comeau could always make him obey her. Jerome did anything Zabeth asked of him, although his obedience was accompanied by a good deal of grumbling.

Perhaps Jerome's cooperation with the two mysterious women was out of respect for their gender rather than any familiarity between them; however, he hated it when anyone spoke to him directly, especially people he did not know. Jerome would often become violent when approached, yet he meekly complied with the women's request to speak with him privately. Is this an indication that Jerome was cooperating out of reverence for old friends or relatives? It has been rumoured Jerome was the brother of one of the women, or both.

While the women never claimed to be related to Jerome, many other people contacted the Comeau family with stories of long-lost brothers and sons. These were still the days of sail and steamships, when being shipwrecked on a foreign shore was not an uncommon end for those who made their living at sea. Jerome's puzzling amputations and his enigmatic silence made his story so compelling that it was reprinted in newspapers around the globe. As a result of the publicity, letters from desperate people searching for lost family members arrived at the Comeau household regularly.

As the years passed, the exchange of letters between the Comeaus and those claiming to be relatives of Jerome generated even more publicity for this sensational story. The December 12, 1898, edition of the *Halifax Herald* boldly, and prematurely, declared the "Jerome mystery of Digby County is about to be solved." The sensational newspaper article relates how the Comeau family received a letter from a woman in Liverpool, England, whose last name was Jerome, who had learned about the legless castaway in a British newspaper. She said she was the sister of the Comeau's house guest. The letter was read to Jerome, who displayed characteristic indifference to the woman's claims. There is no indication if Ms. Jerome of Liverpool ever made further contact with the Comeau family.

Six months later, the *Halifax Morning Chronicle* reported that an Irish woman from New York also claimed to be Jerome's sister. She said her brother had run away from home when he was just twelve, and she believed he was probably the same poor unfortunate man who washed ashore on Digby Neck.

Another such claim arrived from two sisters in New York named Mahoney who were looking for their own brother. Like Jerome their brother was temperamental, and he had run away from home several times as a child. The youngster finally made his escape for good and his family spent the intervening years searching for him. It is possible that these two sisters were the same anonymous women who spoke with Jerome at the Comeau home. A number of theories and stories about Jerome feature a pair of women; it seems likely that the tale of the two mysterious female visitors became jumbled with other recollections over time.

Acadian writer and historian J. Alphonse Deveau wrote a comprehensive article about the Jerome legend in the July 3, 1991, issue of the French newspaper *Le Courrier de la Nouvelle-Écosse*. Deveau relates the story of two women who confronted Charles Comeau, son of Dedier and Zabeth, while he was working in the United States in the late 1890s. They were sisters from Mobile, Alabama, who learned from the shipping registers in the local newspaper that sailors from Nova Scotia were in port. According to the article, the sisters told Charles Comeau that his family's legless house guest was indeed their long-lost brother, Jeremiah Mahoney. Charles later said one of the women resembled Jerome enough to have been his sister.

The two women presented Charles with a sealed envelope along with strict instructions to give the letter directly to Jerome when he returned home. Charles was likely intensely curious, yet he did not tear open the envelope and read the letter. He probably did not maintain the confidentiality of the sealed envelope out of some sense of honour or respect for the privacy of the women or Jerome; it is more likely he didn't know how to read.

As promised, Charles turned the envelope over to Jerome when he returned home, and gave the man a brief explanation of its origins. Jerome clutched the envelope for a few moments, looking at it carefully. He turned it over in his hands several times, then swiftly ripped the thing to pieces and tossed them into the nearby fire.

By the turn of the twentieth century, Jerome had been living with the Comeau family for about thirty years. The prevailing opinion by this time was that Jerome was an Irishman named Mahoney. Other than the unsubstantiated claims of letter writers who said Jerome was their relative, there is little evidence as to why people were so convinced of his Irish origins. George Armstrong was convinced the castaway's name was Matteo. Mahoney and Matteo sound similar enough that if the legless stranger in his delirium mumbled something like Mahoney, it could have been misinterpreted as Matteo. An Irishman named Matthew Mahoney would likely gain the nickname Matty or Maddy, which could easily be mistaken for the Latin-sounding Matteo when muttered by a delirious man.

A tattered clipping from an unidentified New York newspaper, likely printed in late autumn of 1905, refers to the poor Irish settlers in the areas around Clare who could speak Gaelic. The article goes on to say: "There is a strong impression that Gerome's last name is Mahoney, and that he is an Irishman, but he will not respond to any language that is spoken, be it French, Gaelic, Italian, Spanish, German or English." (Note the spelling of Jerome with a *G*.)

The same newspaper clipping relates the story of how a family in New Orleans exchanged letters with the Comeaus about their brother who had run away to the sea at the age of twelve or fourteen. Because of Jerome's age it was very unlikely he was the family's brother, but it is interesting to note that a number of other letter writers also claimed Jerome came from the Southern States. This is not surprising when you consider the South was still recovering from the American Civil War, and many families had not yet come to terms with the loss of their young men in battle.

Among the countless people who visited the Comeau home to view the mysterious Jerome was Judge Alfred William Savary. The distinguished judge played a significant role in Jerome's story, but not because he wanted to claim the castaway as a blood relative. Savary took a special interest in Jerome's case and often called upon the Comeau family as he attended to the county court circuit between Annapolis, Digby, and Yarmouth counties.

But why would a lawyer with an interest in local history be so fascinated by a come-from-away like Jerome? The answer may lie in Savary's upbringing.

Alfred William Savary was born on October 10, 1831, in Plympton, Digby County. He became fluent in French early in life as he travelled up and down the old road along the French Shore with his father. His upbringing among the honest and hard-working Acadians had a strong influence on him. Listening to tales of New France in the native French tongue sparked young Savary's interest in the history of the area. Sad and bitter stories about the Acadian expulsion just over a generation earlier would have awakened young Savary's sense of social justice, steering him toward studying law and entering politics as an adult.

Savary practiced law in New Brunswick before returning to Nova Scotia to hang out his shingle in Digby in 1862. The next year Jerome was found on the beach at Sandy Cove; however, Judge Savary wrote many years later that he did not hear about this remarkable incident until at least a year after Jerome was discovered. It is odd that he did not hear about Jerome immediately after Collie Albright found him on the beach, as news travels fast in a small community, especially news of a story as strange as this. What makes this delay even stranger is that as a lawyer trying to establish a new practice, and as a political candidate, Savary would have travelled extensively around Digby and spoken to many people to drum up support. The early curiosity surrounding Jerome must have died quickly once he was moved to Meteghan and became a familiar fixture in the small community. Savary wrote that his early ignorance of the story "may be explained by the fact that the French people along St. Mary's Bay form a distinct community," that is, they were a close-knit people, and local news didn't travel widely outside of their circle.

Although he first heard about Jerome in 1864, Savary didn't really take the time to research and explore the story in depth until at least the late 1880s, perhaps because he was busy trying to get elected. He was elected the first member of Parliament for Digby in 1867, but lost his seat in 1874. He became a judge of county court in Annapolis, Digby, and Yarmouth Counties in 1876.

Now living in Annapolis, Judge Savary travelled the county court circuit and was able to visit the places he remembered going to as a boy along the French Shore of Clare. It was on his travels as circuit judge that Savary became reacquainted with the strange saga of Jerome. Judge Savary took time from his busy schedule to make detours from his regular route to visit Jerome at the Comeau family home.

For his part, Jerome had little regard for the well-intentioned judge. In the November 17, 1898, *Halifax Herald* newspaper, Judge Savary wrote a letter describing one of his first visits with Jerome:

> I went to see him, and found him the inmate of a respectable Christian home—just as the French always provide for the few paupers they have….The woman of the house told me the facts and the name of himself and his ship, but when he noticed we were talking about him and mentioning his name[,] with a slight frown of reproach he started from the mat on the floor where he was, and crawled out of doors on his hands, dragging his stumps behind him.

The judge did not limit his detective work to simply observing the reluctant Jerome and speaking with his caregivers. He interviewed members of the community, such as the Italian merchant and barber John Meechi. He also personally visited and wrote letters to Jerome's rescuers, Robert Bishop and William Eldridge. He spoke with and wrote to Angus Gidney, by then a successful businessman and provincial politician whose family cared for Jerome before he was sent across the bay to live with Jean Nicola. The persistent judge also maintained a vigorous correspondence with newspapers, colleagues, politicians, and other people of influence in order to relate the story of Jerome and to correct errors in published accounts of his story.

Unlike most writers of the time, Judge Savary was not interested in wild speculation about Jerome's involvement in sinister secret societies, mafia revenge plots, or high-seas piracy. Instead, Savary was driven by an earnest and sincere desire to help the man. Savary believed Jerome deserved respect, and aimed to restore some semblance of dignity to his circus sideshow life by publicly disputing myths, and trying to discover the truth, about Jerome's heritage. Savary expressed his sympathy in a letter to a *New York Herald* journalist in 1906: "[Jerome] most likely had friends or family somewhere who suffered when he did not return, and I regret that an investigation was not made immediately after the event."

In letters to various newspapers, Judge Savary took journalists to task for sensationalizing the story of the poor, unfortunate castaway. He also chastised lazy reporters for not doing some extra digging, as he was, to try to interview the people who actually had a hand in rescuing Jerome. In a letter to the *Saint John Daily Telegraph* on April 1, 1909, Savary wrote:

It is remarkable that newspaper correspondents and others who, lured by the romance and glamour of mystery, look up Jerome and enquire about him never seek to interview those who were familiar with his discovery and saw him soon afterwards…but get accounts of the transaction at second and third hand from people not born or who were mere children at the time, and draw on their own imagination from what that of their informants cannot supply.

Judge Savary originally believed Jerome may have been from Portugal, but in a letter printed on the front page of the *Halifax Herald* on November 17, 1898, Savary confirmed his belief that Jerome was Italian, and a sailor or passenger on an Italian ship "at the time when the inhuman outrage was perpetrated against him." Savary apparently changed his opinion on Jerome's nationality after speaking with John Meechi, the Italian merchant from Meteghan who maintained the mystery man was from Italy. The letter also revealed the judge's disgust at Jerome's treatment and disappointment at the lack of action on the part of the government to bring those who had abandoned Jerome on the beach to justice, writing that it seemed "there could have been no difficulty in finding that ship and solving the mystery if the provincial authorities had followed up that clue. But, apparently they took no interest in the matter whatever."

Judge Savary's observation that no one made a sincere effort to search for the ship could lead a conspiracy-minded person to believe the provincial authorities, as Savary called them, did not want to find it. Perhaps locating the mystery ship would reveal a truth that once uncovered, could not be ignored. People seemed content to allow the mystery of Jerome to remain a mystery.

Savary's frustration with the provincial government's inaction provoked him to take his investigation international, and to contact other countries himself. Among the Annapolis County judge's papers is a letter dated November 28, 1903, from the charge d'affaires of the Italian embassy in Washington, D. C. Unfortunately, the Italian diplomat responded that the matter was out of his jurisdiction and referred Savary to the Italian consul in Halifax and London.

Dedier and Zabeth Comeau were likely impressed by the well-dressed and well-spoken English-speaking judge who came to their door. Judge Savary could also afford to drop more money than regular visitors into the coin box Zabeth kept by the door to encourage donations for Jerome's upkeep. When the Comeaus realized people like Judge Savary would pay for the privilege of seeing Jerome, they saw a unique opportunity to turn a profit.

Chapter 7

The Jerome Show

Dedier and Zabeth may have tolerated the seemingly intolerable Jerome and his many visitors for other reasons besides simple Christian charity. The weekly two-dollar stipend that the provincial government provided for Jerome's care was intended to feed and clothe the poor unfortunate castaway, but with many hungry mouths at their table, Dedier and Zabeth found it hard to resist using the cash for other expenses.

In any large Roman Catholic family at that time there was an expectation, indeed an obligation, that at least one son would enter the priesthood. In the Comeau family, this duty and honour fell to son Enos Jean Comeau who was born July 4, 1881. Young Jean, or Johnie, planned to attend College Sainte-Anne and then enter the seminary. While his parents would have been overwhelmingly proud that he was dedicating his life to the church, they must have struggled with how they were going to pay for his education. The only extra income available to the Comeaus was the government stipend earmarked for Jerome's care. So the decision was easy—Dedier and Zabeth would take the money provided for Jerome and use it to help fund Johnie's schooling.

Dipping into his allotted government stipend was not the only way the Comeaus profited from their boarder. As their home was the local postal stop, it was not unusual for the family to entertain visitors. Many travellers entered the house and made the excuse they were waiting for the stagecoach, when in fact they hoped to catch a glimpse of the legendary Jerome. Zabeth placed a small donation box near the door and encouraged visitors to drop in a coin or two in exchange for a peek at the mystery man. With the regular parade of visitors through their home, passing the hat was the enterprising and practical thing to do.

Every Sunday following church, families flocked to the Comeau home where they were greeted by Zabeth or her children and gently reminded of the donation box near the door. Youngsters enjoyed teasing the volatile oddity from behind the backs of the adults. The parents would then scold their disobedient children and threaten to leave them with Jerome if they didn't behave.

Zabeth claimed the donations she solicited were used to buy clothes and blankets for her house guest. For many of the curiosity seekers who travelled great distances to meet Jerome, a nickel or dime was a small price to pay to view the most famous anonymous man in the world.

After all, Jerome was a bona fide tourist attraction in the small French Acadian village of Saint Alphonse. Jerome generated business for the Dominion Railway, and local hotels and guest houses. Special Jerome sightseeing tours were organized and the Port Royal Hotel in Meteghan, the oldest hotel in the area, hosted countless journalists, politicians, and travellers over the years who, eager to put their individual skills toward solving his mystery, sought out the voiceless enigma. Whenever a ship from overseas would make port in Meteghan, Digby, or nearby Yarmouth, a local would be sent to fetch a sailor to make an obligatory visit to Jerome. The sailor would pepper him with words in his native tongue, hoping Jerome would show some hint of recognition.

The constant parade of gawkers at the Comeau home, while profitable, was also inconvenient and intrusive, prompting Dedier and Zabeth to explore other ways to squeeze money from the worldwide fascination with Jerome. They knew people would pay money to see the puzzling castaway. Jerome was a romantic riddle that captivated the world, and it was only a matter of time before his caregivers caved in to the public pressure to move the show out of their kitchen and entertain ideas to expose the star attraction to a wider audience.

In 1899, Dedier got tangled up in a bizarre scheme to put Jerome on display in a touring sideshow. The first stop was to be McLaughlin's Hall in the ornate building on the corner of Main and Collins streets in the bustling seaport of Yarmouth.

"*Jerome* To Be Exhibited," was the simple, but exciting headline in the June 19, 1899, edition of the *Halifax Morning Chronicle*. The article went on to describe the exhibit: "Jerome, the unfortunate individual whose name has appeared in every Canadian and American newspaper at various times for many years, will…be placed on exhibition in McLaughlin's Hall and will undoubtedly attract a large number of people."

Although Dedier knew the intensely private Jerome would have been horrified to the point of violence at the prospect of being put on display, he became involved with a gentleman named Eleazer Comeau with the Catholic Mutual Benefit Society, who proposed the plan. It appears that the society saw a fundraising opportunity and proposed the unsavoury plot to the Comeaus, who were eager for more income to help finance Johnie's goal of becoming a priest.

The plan made perfect business sense, and seemed infallible. In 1899 Jerome-mania was at a peak. Interest in the mystery man had spanned the globe by this point, and his caregivers likely entertained proposals from more than one shifty entrepreneur looking to cash in. The *Morning Chronicle* eagerly anticipated a lucrative showbiz career for Jerome: "It would not be surprising if Jerome…finds his way to the United States and once there would make a fortune in the various dime museums throughout the country."

The public appetite for human oddities in the so-called civilized world was insatiable at the turn of the last century. Showman P. T. Barnum had thrilled audiences across the United States with his travelling show, which featured the likes of Nova Scotia's giant Angus MacAskill (who died just a few weeks before Jerome appeared on Digby Neck), and the diminutive Tom Thumb, as well as Siamese twins, armless acrobats, fat ladies, and thin men.

Across the ocean, within the seedy sideshows of London, Joseph Merrick captivated the world as the Elephant Man. Merrick was born a normal child one year before Jerome washed up on the beach at Sandy Cove. But as he grew, a rare genetic disorder caused his head and limbs to become strangely deformed, thus earning Merrick his nickname. While he may have been liberated from the circus by Dr. Frederick Treves, Merrick was forced to endure further humiliation when he was put on display as a medical oddity. Like Jerome, the Elephant Man only wanted to be left alone to live his life in peace and quiet dignity.

The Jerome show was to open in July 1899, but it seems that the exhibit never took place, as newspapers of the day make no further mention of it. What could have happened to cancel this surefire hit before opening night? One can only assume Jerome would have no part of it. Jerome was a powerful man. He would not tolerate being forcibly moved from behind his hot wood stove in Saint Alphonse to be put on display in Yarmouth. He undoubtedly would have been violently uncooperative at any attempt to bundle him up for a trip to Yarmouth.

With a defiant performer who refused to perform, his caregivers must have abandoned the scheme to take Jerome on the road. Instead they resigned themselves to continuing to allow visitors into their home, and strongly encouraging a small donation for a chance to peek at supposed royalty.

An endless parade of gawkers, curiosity seekers, and letter writers all eager to stake some claim on the voiceless man continued to visit the Comeau house. It's been said that over the years thousands of people visited the home. Jerome consistently shunned the attention, seeking only to play with the children, and huddle shivering next to the cookstove in the kitchen. When visitors approached him, Jerome either recoiled in disgust, or lashed out violently, growling like a dog. He reportedly snarled, "I'll bite you," to an approaching stranger at least once.

The dark depression that gripped Jerome likely deepened in the late 1890s, when Dedier and Zabeth announced they were moving. While Dedier was a modest man, his house had to be large enough to accommodate his typically abundant Catholic family. The Comeau family had grown too large for their first home, so Dedier built another up the hill.

The new home was ready to move into by 1902. While the family gathered up their belongings in anticipation of starting life in their new home, Jerome sullenly refused to budge. He hated change. For all he knew he was being shipped off and abandoned again, perhaps just when he was beginning to trust the kind family caring for him. After over thirty years in the house, Jerome had to be forcibly removed. Dragged the short distance across the road, the legless man put up a fight when they tried to make him enter his new home. It is said that once they managed to wrestle him inside, Jerome never ventured outdoors again.

Struggling with an uncooperative Jerome seemed to be a regular occurrence for the men in the Comeau household, and Dedier knew what his boarder was capable of. He was a powerful man prone to violent outbursts. Even able-bodied men had trouble restraining Jerome when he was angry.

On one occasion, an American newspaper reporter arrived on the Comeaus' doorstep looking to meet Jerome. As was the custom for visitors seeking an audience with the castaway, the journalist brought a gift of tobacco and candy. When the gentleman approached Jerome to make his offering, the silent man became visibly enraged. "The crimson tide arose from his neck and flooded his face to the roots of his hair," wrote the reporter.

When a member of the Comeau family tried to force Jerome to take the reporter's gift, he let out a terrible scream and beat viciously at the hands extended to him. The reporter wrote that in

Jerome's "gesture and cry of repulsion against the familiar friend there was no bitterness, no brutal sullenness, only the sensitive resentment of a high-strung nature."

For a seasonal labourer like Dedier, the guaranteed annual income of Jerome's government stipend, plus the regular admission fees charged to visitors would have helped ease any doubts he had about caring for Jerome, no matter how unpredictable and unpleasant he became. But Dedier never completely trusted his house guest. He refused to leave Jerome alone in the house with women and girls. He may have been trying to protect his wife and daughters from physical harm by ensuring a man was always present.

In 1902, shortly after building his new home, Dedier passed away. Some said the strain of building the house led to his death. The death of her husband left Zabeth truly alone for the first time since she married Dedier in 1862. Her children were growing and slowly moving out of the family home. By this time daughter Marie Amee may have been married. Son Jean was preparing for the priesthood, Charles was constantly travelling, and William was married and living in the United States.

Zabeth was a strong, proud Acadian woman. Her robust character, coupled with her unwavering Catholic faith, should have been the pillars she needed to face life as a widow, yet Zabeth wavered. She sent a letter to her son William in the United States begging him to return home. What prompted the confident Zabeth to make such a desperate appeal to her son living so far away? Could it be Zabeth pleaded with her son to return because she was afraid of being left alone with Jerome?

Soon the dutiful son William returned to Nova Scotia, bringing his American bride with him. Like Jerome, the young woman found herself an outsider in a strange country among people speaking a foreign language, living in a close-knit community that she was not a part of. Adding to her isolation was the fact that she was a Presbyterian, putting her at odds with the staunchly Roman Catholic family and village she found herself in.

William's wife became intimate with the details of Jerome's story—sparse though they were—as she was called upon to act as interpreter whenever an anglophone journalist or visitor seeking to learn more about the legless castaway called on the French household. She likely relished the frequent American visitors to the Comeau home, who not only provided her with the opportunity to speak English, but also to glean some news from her home country.

William's wife also corroborated a fascinating detail in this tangled tale during a conversation at her physician's office in the early twentieth century. One day she travelled to Yarmouth for a visit with Dr. Charles Webster, a well-respected physician. She was something of a curiosity in the doctor's office, since she came from along the French Acadian shore, but was quite obviously an anglophone. Dr. Webster's wife, Mary Paige, offered the woman a cup of tea and the two sat for a chat. The woman explained how she had moved from the United States to live with her husband's family in Clare.

The conversation soon turned to Jerome, and Mrs. Comeau told Mrs. Webster about the peculiar legless man. She then casually mentioned that late at night when he thought others were asleep, the silent man would open his mouth and sing in a low, mournful voice, in a strange foreign language. Despite his refusal to speak openly to adults and only grumbling or growling when forced to respond to a question, it seems Jerome had a beautiful singing voice. Nearly a century later, the story of the American woman's visit and her tale of Jerome's pitiful song is still told within the Webster family.

As the years progressed, Jerome's youthful appearance faded. His fine and delicate hands, thought by some to be a symbol of his nobility, withered and wasted in his lap. His hair whitened and the wrinkles of age crept across his face. Zabeth, and then her granddaughters, kept his hair and moustache trimmed and cut his beard in the stylish Van Dyck fashion popular among Frenchmen at the time.

Jerome never thanked his caregivers during the decades he spent in the Comeau home. It appears there may have been a mutual distrust between Jerome and Dedier Comeau when he was alive. While Jerome quite obviously hated to be put on display and prodded by the questions and staring eyes of strangers, the

Comeaus were intent on allowing any visitor easy access to their house guest.

Jerome must have known the Comeaus were at least partially motivated to care for him by their dependence on the regular income his plight provided. It may be too damning to attribute the Comeaus' hospitality to greed, but there seemed to be little compunction over appropriating the money meant for Jerome for other family expenses, such as Johnie's education. Indeed, spending the money to allow their son to enter the priesthood was likely seen as a more genuine way to perform the Lord's will.

The Comeau family genuinely cared for Jerome, and their approval of the constant parade of gawkers was due in part to their eagerness to solve the mystery of the legless castaway, which might allow him to return to his former life. The family openly shared Jerome's story with visitors and invited any attempts from others to shed light on his background, yet their house guest certainly did not appreciate these efforts.

For her part, Zabeth felt her primary duty toward Jerome and to her faith, was to ensure the silent man would be able to enjoy all the benefits of everlasting life. While she must have been very curious about solving the mystery of her house guest, she was more compelled by her responsibility to her church. As Jerome grew older, Zabeth's thoughts turned to ensuring Jerome would be baptized so that he would die and be buried a Roman Catholic. It was later reported Zabeth's son Charles believed his mother somehow knew more about the true story of the mystery of Jerome than she revealed. If Zabeth had heard Jerome's confession, this is a secret she took to her grave.

Chapter 8

The Frozen Man

Like the world-famous tides in St. Mary's Bay, interest in the mystery of Jerome at times rose to remarkable heights only to ebb to practically nothing. Jerome enjoyed a few months of relative peace every few years when the parade of curious visitors and gawkers slowed to a trickle, but then another newspaper would rediscover his story and publish large headlines about the human sphinx living in the remote Nova Scotian village. Often, the new reports were sparked by yet another letter sent to the Comeaus by some lonely soul claiming, or hoping, Jerome was a long-lost son or brother.

Indulging in the Jerome mystery seemed to be a favourite pastime for many people. Each article prompted armchair sleuths to concoct fantastic theories about the mystery man. With no new facts to enliven the story and Jerome's refusal to cooperate with newspaper reporters, interest in the story always eventually faded again.

By late 1905, Jerome had lived quietly among the Clare Acadians for over forty years. At that time, several Canadian and American newspapers revisited his strange story. These new headlines likely prompted a number of reporters from New York City newspapers to descend upon the Comeau home in Saint Alphonse with the goal of using their big-city investigative skills to solve Jerome's mystery. The first New York journalist on the scene had trouble finding anyone who could confirm if Jerome actually still lived in the area, proving that the locals had lost interest in the story by that time. While sailing from Boston to Yarmouth aboard the steamer *Prince George*, the reporter spoke with a Captain McKinnon and his crew, but the sailors barely remembered the story. Once docked in Yarmouth the reporter struck out again with the agent for the Dominion Railway, who had actually worked in Meteghan for a year but did not know who Jerome was. Luckily for the New Yorker, "there were some loungers about the wharf who had (heard of Jerome), and said the man would be found sure enough if one inquired along the country road."

The Yankee reporter finally succeeded in meeting Jerome face to face, but if he hoped to write the final chapter in the story, he was disappointed. The reporter summed up his quest quite eloquently:

> And so the secret of Jerome is likely to go with him to the grave, and no one will ever know what tragedy preceded the anchoring of that strange vessel in St. Mary's Bay so many years ago. Death and distance are the only abyss which yawn between human lives. Here is a gulf, whether of anguish or remorse, too deep for fathoming.

While the article failed to reveal the secret behind the mystery of Jerome, it did generate even more interest in the story. The next year, in 1906, a reporter from the *New York Herald* visited Nova Scotia with two companions. The group travelled to Meteghan to seek out the mysterious "Gerome," as they spelled it. Though Jerome had remained silent for over forty years, these New Yorkers had the grandiose ambition that they might succeed, in one visit, in getting Jerome to talk even though so many others had failed.

Jerome did not oblige. The Americans would have gone away with nothing new to add to the story if not for a chance conversation with their stagecoach driver. For many years the coachman was a neighbour of a Mrs. Doucet, a former schoolteacher. When the driver told Mrs. Doucet about the American visitors and their interest in Jerome, the woman admitted she was Madeleine Genevieve, daughter of Julitte Comeau and stepdaughter of Jean Nicola, the

Russian. Now fifty-six years old and eager to talk about her friend, Madeleine Genevieve revealed for the reporter an intimate and very personal account of living with Jerome.

The loving friendship between Jerome and Madeleine had continued long after she grew into adulthood and Jerome moved away. After not seeing each other for many years, Jerome had greeted Madeleine with recognition and affection when she visited him one day at the Comeaus' home.

It did not take much for the Americans to persuade Madeleine Genevieve to return with them to the Comeau house the next day. She had not seen Jerome for ten years and was anxious to visit her childhood playmate.

Madeleine Genevieve entered the kitchen where Jerome was in his customary position, huddled close to the hot stove, head bowed with hands in his lap. As she bent near him to say *bonjour*, the unpredictable Jerome drew back and angrily raised his hand as if to swat away another intrusion into his solitude.

Unafraid, Madeleine knelt close and tenderly asked, "Don't you know me anymore Gerome?" Jerome looked her in the face and a glimmer of recognition appeared. But he knew that the reporter was watching him, and quickly cast his glance downward.

"Why don't you talk to me Gerome?" she pleaded. He pitifully mumbled something and Madeleine asked him to speak louder. Jerome then turned to face his friend in an effort to be clearly understood. Again he mumbled a few words that Madeleine interpreted as *je ne peux pas,* meaning "I cannot." The reporter declared that after so many years of silence, Jerome's vocal cords were no longer capable of speech. With his voice lost forever, it was useless to question him further.

This account appeared in the *New York Herald* on Sunday, December 9, 1906, and was reprinted in other major newspapers across the United States and Canada. Thrust again into the spotlight, the Jerome mystery generated numerous letters to various newspaper editors.

While the *New York Herald* declared the mystery of Jerome unsolvable, a storm of controversy was quietly brewing on the pages of the smaller local papers of Nova Scotia and New Brunswick. It wasn't the dauntless detective work of big-city reporters that was causing the stir, but some quiet concerns expressed in a letter to the editor of the local newspaper.

Though the American reporters' renewed interest in Jerome was likely sparked by the flurry of new headlines, in their rush to crack the case they overlooked a crucial piece of information that appeared in the *Yarmouth Herald* on September 18, 1905, and was reprinted in the *Digby Courier* a few days later on September 22. The item was a letter to the editor from a gentleman named C. O. Foss, the assistant district engineer for the Transcontinental Railway in Fredericton, New Brunswick. Foss is yet another in the list of prominent, influential people compelled to get involved in the mystery of Jerome. Foss went on to become chief engineer and one of the first commissioners of the New Brunswick Power Commission, forerunner of NB Power.

At that time the railroad was being built through Chipman, New Brunswick, and Foss was working on the project. In his letter to the editor, Foss said he had read an article in the *Saint John Sun,* evidently reprinted from a newspaper in Boston, about the mystery man of Meteghan a few days earlier. Foss happened to be sitting next to an elderly gentleman with whom he shared the article, and the pair started talking about Jerome. The fellow, described as "past 70, and a man of most trustworthy authority," told Mr. Foss he knew the history behind this mystery man.

The elderly gentleman told Mr. Foss an amazing, yet sad story that suggested Jerome wasn't a prince or a prisoner, but the victim of near tragedy and neglect. The story did not begin on the high seas, but in the backwoods of New Brunswick, with a confused, freezing young foreigner stumbling through the trees in the middle of winter. The gentleman went on to explain to Mr. Foss how he believed the story of the man known as Jerome had begun:

Some 46 or 47 years ago [in 1858 or 1859], two brothers by the name of Conroy, lumbermen…found a strange man lying on one of his timber brows, a place where lumbermen roll logs into the stream, on the bank of the Gaspereau River, 20 miles from here [Chipman, New Brunswick]. This person was very near perishing, both of his legs being badly frozen. They brought him here and he was taken in charge by the parish authorities. It was found that to finally save his life it would be necessary to amputate both his legs. So he was taken to Gagetown...where a Dr. Peters of local fame in those days as a surgeon, performed the operation. The man recovered, and...was brought back here where he was supported for a period of nearly two years as a parish charge, he lived in the home of a family named Galligher.

The gentleman told Foss that the frozen man was given the name Gamby, because he made noises that sounded like that. After a time, the man called Gamby became too much of a burden for the community, and he was "taken to St. John and there an arrangement was made with some schooner captain to take him across (the Bay of Fundy) and leave him in Nova Scotia." The elderly gentleman added that it was "well known who took him from here, but the exact arrangement about his transportation across the Bay is not known, only the fact that he was taken and left there."

Could this shocking story be true? Were the frozen man cast out of New Brunswick and Jerome the same person? In an indictment of the actions of his fellow New Brunswickers, Mr. Foss wrote: "It seems quite certain that the people hereabouts were not as kindly hospitable as the simple Acadian fisherfolk of Digby County, for even the parish authorities were determined to be rid of the helpless unfortunate."

The "trustworthy authority" left Mr. Foss with the impression that the story of the frozen man known as Gamby was familiar to the people of Chipman in 1905. It was also obvious that the elderly gentleman believed that Gamby was the man who later washed up on the beach at Sandy Cove and became known as Jerome. He felt that the people of Chipman remembered how this man was sent across the Bay of Fundy and "left there," yet this information had remained concealed for nearly half a century.

How is it so many people believed for so long that Jerome may have been a prince or pirate, or that his secret was guarded by some sinister secret society, if indeed the truth could be found in a small town in nearby New Brunswick? It seems that the evidence to support this story may have been ignored rather than hidden. Old newspaper clippings and the private papers of researchers like Judge Alfred William Savary reveal that the evidence connecting Jerome to Gamby was available from the time he arrived on Digby Neck. As it turns out, the rumour that Jerome was an injured woodsman from New Brunswick *was* being whispered in 1863, and even popped up in the newspapers before Foss wrote his letter in 1905.

Judge Savary, who had been studying Jerome's case for years, likely read Foss's letter when it appeared in the *Digby Courier* or when it was reprinted in the *Yarmouth Herald*. The remarkable story, and the allegation that the people of Chipman, New Brunswick, had abandoned the helpless stranger who later became known as

Jerome would have come as no surprise to Judge Savary—he had heard the story before. But Savary didn't believe the tale contained in the letter. In fact, he had dismissed the claim as false over ten years earlier. In 1893, the *Digby Courier* printed a letter from a Mr. W. Wilson of Cambridge, Queen's County, New Brunswick. In his letter Wilson, like Foss, states the frozen man whose legs were amputated in New Brunswick must be Jerome. Wilson's claim was refuted by Judge Savary, in a response written to the *Digby Courier* on September 22, 1893. Savary shoots down the possibility of a connection between Jerome and the frozen man in New Brunswick, saying Wilson is "surely mistaken in his supposed identification of the man whom he speaks of."

It is difficult to understand why Savary was so certain that Jerome was not the same man who was found nearly frozen to death in the New Brunswick woods. It may have been because there was a question about the condition of Jerome's amputation scars at the time he was found on Digby Neck. Savary believed the popular legend that Jerome's wounds were fresh, and that his stumps had barely healed when he was discovered. Savary's feeling that Jerome's legs were amputated just before he was discovered on the beach would have made it impossible to believe that he was the fellow who was operated on in New Brunswick several years earlier.

Perhaps the fair-minded judge simply could not comprehend how this "inhuman outrage," as he called it, was allowed to happen to a helpless amputee. After all, as a young lawyer Savary practiced in New Brunswick and likely thought very highly of his friends there. Savary's strong feelings echo the words that Justice of the Peace George Armstrong wrote over forty-five years earlier, just days after the discovery of Jerome in Sandy Cove. Armstrong's letter, printed under the accusing headline "Barbarity" in the *Christian Messenger* newspaper on October 7, 1863, said: "What barbarity, inhumanity, cruelty and injustice does this act show in the perpetrators!"

As noted earlier, Armstrong's letter is the first eyewitness account of Jerome in the days after his rescue on Digby Neck. The editor of the *Christian Messenger* added a curious postscript to the letter that was, for some reason, overlooked for many years. The postscript reveals a rumour that circulated at the time about a person matching Jerome's description:

> We remember seeing, in a New Brunswick paper, a week or two since, an account of the removal of a person exactly similar to the unfortunate stranger mentioned in the above, from some part of their province. The person who took him in charge was paid, as we understood, to take him to New York or Boston, that he might be sent thence to his own country.

Obviously, the man did not make it to either of those large seaports as he was dumped unceremoniously on the shores of Nova Scotia. The editor's postscript also had some harsh words for those responsible: "Such shameful barbarity, but little less than murder, if parties concerned can be discovered should be severely punished."

It is not known why this telling postscript was overlooked and a follow-up investigation not conducted immediately. Had enquiries been made in New Brunswick at the time, the mystery of the legless, voiceless castaway might have been solved right then and there. Any interprovincial enquiries that may have been made in 1863 would likely have been met with denials and feigned ignorance. It seems those people responsible for casting out Jerome must have felt considerable guilt and shame at what they had done. Perhaps the people who arranged for the removal of the legless man tried to cover up their actions, especially after it was discovered he did not make it to New York or Boston, but was cruelly abandoned on a remote beach.

Despite the judge's intransigence, by September 1905 the connection between Jerome and the man known as Gamby was becoming difficult to deny. With renewed attention on Jerome's case, it was only a matter of time before the media started poking around Chipman, New Brunswick. It fell to the venerable Senator George Gerald King, a lumber baron and the area's leading citizen of the day, to confirm or deny the growing rumour about the actions some of his townspeople had taken many years before.

Senator G. G. King is wound tightly within the fabric of Chipman's history. To many, he is considered the founder of Chipman as a centre for business. King was first elected to Parliament in 1878, but lost his seat in a controversial election in 1887. In 1891, King regained his seat as member of Parliament, was re-elected again in 1896, and was one of the first people appointed to the Senate by Sir Wilfred Laurier.

Chipman prospered under King's leadership. With his keen mind, King molded the area's rough and ready lumberjacks into an industrious labour force. His sawmill not only churned out lumber, but shingles, lathes, and other wood products. As his holdings increased, the King Lumber Company came to control a number of logging camps embedded in the thick forests that enveloped Chipman. King may have inherited control of some of these logging camps from his father. One of these remote logging camps was perched along the banks of the Gaspereau River, which flows not far from the outskirts of the village.

In an article published in the *Saint John Daily Sun* on September 16, 1905, Senator King made an unapologetic confession. Indeed, the man once known as Gamby had been cast out of New Brunswick after being cared for by the residents of Chipman. After his legs were amputated, the man was sent downriver by steamer to the port of Saint John. The article reported that the senator tried to absolve Chipman somewhat by suggesting the people of Saint John shared some of the blame for Jerome's terrible fate:

> Senator King says he is not sure whether it was at the insistence of the Saint John authorities or the Chipman people

that the man was sent away from the province, but he recalls the fact that he was put on board a coasting schooner and taken to Nova Scotia, where he was inhumanly abandoned, a helpless waif, legless, and speechless as far as coherent utterance was concerned.

Despite trying to keep silent on the embarrassing matter for nearly half a century, the people of Chipman could no longer ignore their role in the affair that happened in 1859, early in the village's history.

Chapter 9

The Burden

In 1859, Chipman was barely even a town. It was merely a small notch hacked out of the dense woods that rose like walls on each side of Salmon River, a few kilometres upriver from the head of Grand Lake. Isolated by the impenetrable forest, the only route to or from the outpost was the river. In the harsh New Brunswick winter, even this narrow river highway became impassable, totally cutting off the inhabitants from civilization until the spring thaw.

Like many communities in the deep woods of New Brunswick, the parish of Chipman sprouted up around a sawmill. A strong arm was needed to cut the trees, and the boys of Chipman grew up rough, tough, and able to swing an axe. Life in the isolated backwoods was equally rough and tough. The lumbermen were a hard-living lot, and their way of life could seem disturbingly severe to outsiders.

Piecing together Jerome's story prior to his discovery on the brow of logs is an exercise in guesswork and informed speculation. It was believed the young man was briefly employed at a lumber camp near Chipman, one of many that dotted the interior of the province. After being named to the Senate, it was reported that G. G. King remembered that one of the local lumber camps, perhaps one controlled by his father, was visited by the odd foreigner who was later found nearly frozen to death on the brow of logs in the river one cold winter.

Jerome must have walked into one of these camps by foot. It seems these would be among the last steps his feet would ever take. Some later writers assumed that he had arrived in New Brunswick by boat and may have jumped ship after docking at the port of Chatham. The stranger who arrived at the logging camp was likely making his way from Chatham to the open winter port of Saint John to sign on with another ship.

Travel in the backwoods of New Brunswick in winter was uncomfortable for those who had the luxury of a horse-drawn sleigh, but on foot the journey could be deadly. In areas where the distance between roadhouses was lengthy, unprepared travellers on foot risked frostbite and exposure. Jerome may have arrived at the logging camp in order to find shelter before continuing his winter journey. It is also likely he was looking for some work to subsidize the rest of his trek to Saint John.

Jerome was an outsider, speaking a foreign language, and did not seem to make any friends. It was December 1859, and with Christmas at hand many of the woodsmen had left the lumber camp to enjoy a short visit with their families. With few men around to provide companionship, and language differences making it impossible to communicate with those left to care for the horses, the lonely stranger may have occupied himself by exploring the woods and walking along the Gaspereau River or the banks of Cain's River, not far from the logging camp.

After a short time at the camp, he disappeared. Likely no one noticed when he failed to return to his bunk one bitterly cold night. Perhaps it was thought the stranger had simply moved on down the road as transient labourers often do.

Winter in the lumber woods was not an easy time for hardy, experienced woodsmen, let alone a foreigner from a warmer European climate—and the winter of 1859 was especially brutal. Anyone unlucky enough to get lost in the woods without shelter all night would almost certainly have perished.

While walking along the Gaspereau River, Jerome ran into serious, potentially deadly, trouble. He may have been trying to cross the water by gingerly balancing on some logs that had been floated into place, or he may have gotten lost in the darkness and stepped out onto some thin ice at the edge of the river. Whatever led to it, Jerome took a terrible misstep and plunged into the icy water.

Hypothermia would have seized him almost immediately. As he struggled to claw his way over the logs and on to the riverbank, his hands quickly must have become stiff, numb, and useless. Kicking himself up and out of the water was nearly impossible as the muscles in his soaked legs became sluggish. Had he remained immersed in the frigid river for more than a few minutes, he almost certainly would have died. But in his desperation, Jerome frantically pulled himself out of the water and onto the brow of logs.

Hypothermia causes confusion, loss of balance, and impaired judgment. It is very possible he was suffering from mild hypothermia even before he fell into the water. Perhaps his confused hypothermic state is the reason he was wandering alone in the forest in the first place.

The empty woods swallowed his cries for help and screams of shock. His violent shivering would have eased and his desperate gasps for breath would have become even shallower as his body slowly shut down. Deep confusion must have clouded his shocked mind. Perhaps he was awarded some measure of mercy from his suffering by hallucinating that he was back home, across the sea among family and friends. In this stupor, Jerome may have mouthed a few quiet words of goodbye to his loved ones as his body prepared for death.

This is where Jerome's story should have ended—a confused foreigner, unaccustomed to the harsh Canadian winter, who gets lost in the thick, nearly impassable forest and succumbs to the deadly cold. Freezing to death alone in the New Brunswick lumber woods, as gruesome as it seems today, was not altogether uncommon in the mid-1800s. New Brunswick newspapers often carried short notices of those who had perished in the woods from exposure. Had this been the man's fate, his death may have merited a mention in the newspaper, a few lines at most, then he would have been forgotten, never to be thought of or puzzled over.

Instead, Jerome was tougher than most. He survived. He clung to life despite the cruellest conditions. His survival against the odds was probably partly due to his regularly robust health, but also his soon-to-be famed stubbornness and obstinate refusal to die.

According to one version of the story, the stranger was discovered the next morning sprawled across the brow of logs, having spent the freezing night outside exposed to the elements. Despite his legendary constitution, it seems unlikely the man could have survived outdoors in the middle of winter while soaking wet. Another version of his discovery contends the foreigner managed to drag his nearly frozen body back to the lumber camp where he spent the night shivering in a sawmill. While an unheated sawmill would scarcely have been any warmer than the outdoors, it would at least have provided the hypothermic stranger with protection from the chilling wind.

Regardless of where the frozen, nearly dead man spent the night, he would not have survived much longer were it not for two brothers who stumbled across him that frigid December morning. Daniel and Vernon Conroy were lumbermen themselves who worked the woods along the Gaspereau River. The brothers knew these woods as well as anyone could, and they were well aware of the dangers of the life they led. While the circumstances were dire, it is somehow delightfully coincidental that the two times Jerome was hovering close to death, a pair of brothers who made an accidental early-morning discovery saved him. In 1863 it was the curious Albright brothers who happened upon the dazed Jerome on the Sandy Cove beach and prevented him from being washed away by the highest tides in the world. But prior to this, the Conroy brothers rescued Jerome from nearly freezing to death.

While most accounts only credit the two Conroy brothers with the discovery of the frozen foreigner, there is evidence the pair were part of a larger party of lumbermen. The gang may have been marching out of the woods to return to their families for Christmas when they came upon the frozen man. Another member of this group was a man named Peter Garvey. His name was first mentioned in connection with the discovery of the frozen man in a letter from a resident of Chipman to the editor of the *Saint John Daily Telegraph*, printed April 5, 1909. Notwithstanding the incorrect date for the frozen man's discovery, the letter states: "About the year 1857, Peter Garvey engaged in lumbering, went to the lumber brow with a load of logs. Lying under the end of the logs, as they lay on the ice in Gaspereaux River, he found a man so severely frozen that he was nearly helpless."

When the men came upon the pale, still body of the young man, they likely did not expect to find any signs of life. His clothing would have been stiff as ice having frozen overnight. To their surprise the man was alive, but barely. The group bundled up the man and prepared him for the journey to the nearest outpost of civilization—the remote, forest-bound village of Chipman.

After arriving in Chipman, the injured, incoherent foreigner enters into the official records of New Brunswick for the first time. A series of bills, receipts, and invoices provide actual written evidence of what happened to the stranger later identified as Jerome, and how he was treated in the months following his accident. The records of the Overseers of the Poor of Chipman reveal a sad story of rejection for the stranger dubbed the frozen man, as they trace the path of an unwelcome burden passed from house to house in the village. The Overseers of the Poor of the Parish of Chipman was the committee of local citizens charged with the responsibility of making sure the destitute within their parish boundaries were clothed, fed, and housed. In the early 1860s, the Overseers of Poor consisted of the distinguished gentlemen John O'Leary, George Bennison, and Samuel White.

What could have caused the good people of this small New Brunswick village to consider the drastic step they took against the crippled foreigner? A thorough examination of the organization's ledgers and invoices paints an increasingly disturbing picture of a community pushed to commit a desperate act because of a burden they didn't feel they deserved.

Many of the records relating to the frozen man gathered dust for years in storage in Gagetown. They might have remained there, and the full story of the frozen man, and the evidence linking him to Jerome, would never have been discovered if it were not for the thorough detective work of Dr. Frederic Addison McGrand (1895–1988). According to documents held by the Queens County Historical Society, Dr. McGrand tracked down these bills and invoices and, in "a fine job of preservation," made sure they were properly catalogued and filed with the New Brunswick Provincial Archives in Fredericton.

Dr. McGrand is another prominent politician who took an active interest in the story of Jerome. He was an avid historian who served as New Brunswick's minister of health and was appointed to the Senate of Canada in 1955. One of his main research areas was the link between cruelty to animals and the tendency of humans to commit inhumane or violent acts against each other. The mistreatment that Jerome received at the hands of his caregivers in New Brunswick must have held some fascination for Dr. McGrand.

Of the documents collected by Dr. McGrand, likely during the 1960s, the first to refer to the frozen man was a bill forwarded to the Overseers of the Poor. The bill was for money owing to a gentleman named John Brown, who took care of the frozen man and delivered him to the Overseers of the Poor:

Queens County to
John Brown

For keeping a foreigner, who was insane and indignant and frozen, for 5 days, and for taking him to the overseers of the poor in the year 1859 – £2

It is not certain if Brown was a member of the Conroys' lumber party, or if the brothers delivered the injured man to him. Jerome's near-death experience, along with the shock of being plunged into an icy river left him incomprehensible. In this state, it is no wonder he was labelled "insane." At the first opportunity, John Brown relieved himself of his burden and deposited the foreigner with George Bennison, as the next bill shows:

Parish of Chipman.
To George Bennison. 1860.

To one weeks board and
care towards keeping a frozen man   £1 – 4 – 6
A shirt and drawers   £0 – 10 – 0

Bennison took care of the frozen man for a week and mercifully made sure the poor soul had a clean pair of underwear. New clothes were something the people of Chipman could easily provide, but they had to look beyond the borders of their village to deal with the problem of the man's injured legs.

His legs never recovered from being severely frozen that night in late 1859. Once frozen, the tissue likely turned necrotic. The dead tissue was a risk for further infection, and even gangrene. His legs, rotting beneath him, gave off the horrible smell of decaying flesh. Something had to be done about his useless, rotting legs.

Amputation was the only solution, but the vital surgery did not happen right away. The decision to amputate a frostbitten limb is usually postponed until the area has had a chance to heal and the dead tissue can be more easily identified. Removing frostbitten appendages would have been routine for many New Brunswick doctors during this period. Toes and fingers were regularly lopped off unlucky travellers who had gotten caught in a cold snap along the back roads. Even when a doctor was not available there were other, less professional, methods to deal with frostbitten body parts.

In 1827 a fellow named Thomas Dodds was travelling from his home in Nipisiguit to the Miramichi when, like Jerome, he ran into some bitterly cold weather. His feet were so severely frozen that his companion had to chop off his toes with a mallet and chisel.

As C. O. Foss learned from the elderly gentleman that day in 1905, the man had to be moved again, this time to Gagetown for his amputation surgery. While amputation may have been routine for the physician or the person holding the chisel, it could be unbearably painful for the patient. A few swigs of rum and a thick strap of leather to bite into were traditionally the only painkillers available to someone facing such a surgery in the backwoods. Jerome would have been extremely lucky if he had been brought to Dr. Martin Hunter Peters, well respected as a resourceful and skillful surgeon who made New Brunswick medical history when he performed the first surgery using general anesthetic in that province in 1847.

But was Dr. Martin Hunter Peters the same Dr. Peters who operated on Jerome? According to Dr. Frederic Addison McGrand, it was the famous Dr. Martin Hunter Peters who performed the surgery. This belief is supported by another noted historian, Dr. W. Brenton Stewart, author of the exhaustive *Medicine in New Brunswick—A History of the Practice of Medicine in the Province of New Brunswick.* In his book, Dr. Stewart delves into the Jerome mystery in some detail, asserting it was Dr. Martin H. Peters who removed his legs.

However, another less well-known Dr. Peters was operating in the Gagetown area at this time. The name Peters is closely entwined with the early development of Gagetown, and more than one Dr. Peters practiced medicine in the area over the years. It is the name of Dr. Harry Peters, who lived in Gagetown and died in 1865, that is written across the top of the bill for the surgery on a patient who is obviously the frozen man. The bill reads:

1861. Parish of Chipman.
The Overseers of the Poor for the Parish of Chipman.

Dr. Harry Peters. MD.
For professional attendance and medications for an Italian calling himself, "Ellerimo," in March, April and May, 1861, including fee for amputating both of his legs.

£25 − 0 − 0.

It is unfortunate that for so many years Dr. Harry Peters has been denied recognition for his role in the celebrated story of Jerome, especially since many commentators have acknowledged that Jerome's amputations were skillfully done by a very talented surgeon.

What manner of patient must Jerome have been? As a caregiver to hard-living and heavy-boozing lumbermen, Dr. Peters was probably accustomed to dealing with difficult people. If Jerome's later attitude and behaviour are any indication, he was likely an unruly patient. When faced with the uncooperative foreigner, Dr. Harry Peters would have been very grateful for the calming effects of the ether Dr. Martin Peters introduced to New Brunswick physicians over ten years earlier.

As difficult as the frozen man likely was, Dr. Peters recognized the seriousness of his injuries and the urgent need to remove the afflicted limbs as soon as possible. After ensuring the struggling patient was strapped down and effectively anesthetized, Dr. Peters cut into the damaged tissue.

Dr. Peters could have finished amputating each leg in as little as fifteen minutes. Within a half-hour, Jerome became a double-amputee. Though the surgery was complete, the potential for infection and complications still posed a danger to the patient. Antiseptics were not yet used in surgery, and many physicians did not bother to clean their surgical instruments between operations, let alone wash their own hands.

Following the surgery, Jerome recuperated at the home of John Hutchinson in Gagetown from March until May 1861. As the county jailer, Hutchinson was accustomed to dealing with hostile customers, so the difficult amputee should have been no problem. Once he was well enough to travel, and Dr. Peters was satisfied his amputations were healing properly, the frozen man was shipped back to Chipman. Unable to support himself, the foreigner was again thrust upon the Overseers of the Poor.

Being shuffled around from place to place and house to house, like an unwelcome stray animal, would cause deep resentment in all but the most stable of minds. Given this treatment early in his history, it is little wonder Jerome displayed such moodiness when being passed among families on Digby Neck, and then on to Clare.

The bill for the amputation surgery identifies the frozen man as an Italian with a name that sounds like Ellerimo. Because he was thought to be Italian, it was assumed that he was a Roman Catholic, the same assumption made a few years later on Digby Neck. The Overseers of the Poor arranged to place the legless foreigner in the local Catholic household of Phillip Gallagher, his brother, George, and their family. In the 1861 census, a "cripple" called Lemo Billemy or Bellemy is listed as a lodger with the family of "Phillip Galligher, farmer."

But it was not by the name Ellerimo, or Lemo—or Aleramo as more recent researchers suggest—that Jerome was known in Chipman. Here, they called him Gamby. He gained this nickname after a seemingly nonsense sound he often repeated. At the time it was thought he could have been saying Gambia. It was not until many years later that a reasonable explanation for the word was put forward by Yarmouth historian Arthur Thurston, who made the connection that *gamba* is the Italian word meaning "leg."

When the poor frozen man repeated the word *gamba*, he was sorrowfully and painfully calling out for his lost legs. Perhaps he did not understand what had been done to him. When his caregivers took to calling him Gamby, the confused amputee may have thought they were mocking him over the loss of his legs.

From the start, the committee of gentlemen who made up the Chipman Overseers of the Poor insisted that the man they called Gamby was not their responsibility. After all, he was not a citizen of Chipman. He was found deep in the woods, and the lumbermen who rescued him could not say for certain in which county or parish they picked him up. The committee even tried to shift the burden to their neighbours by claiming the frozen man had been found in adjacent Northumberland County, not Queens. He just happened to be dragged to Chipman because it was the closest outpost of civilization, and the lumber party that rescued him was heading in that direction.

Between 1861 and 1862, the Overseers begged the provincial government for financial support to defray the escalating cost of supporting Gamby. In 1862, the members of a committee expressed the townspeople's growing frustration over the use of their tax dollars in a letter to Lieutenant-Governor Arthur Hamilton Gordon in 1862:

> Now he is a heavy charge on said parish, the inhabitants of which feel dissatisfied that they have to support a man, whose maladies did not happen in their parish nor was he picked up there. A man who was picked up many miles from them and by misadventure imposed on them Frozen and Decripped, a Stranger, a Foreigner, whose language the people cannot understand.

Perhaps no members of the community were more dissatisfied with Gamby than Phillip Gallagher and his family. The gentleman farmer took in the poor frozen man out of Christian charity toward a fellow Catholic, but his generosity had limits. While Gamby had no legs, it seems he had busy hands. In what today might be considered a case of sexual harassment, Gamby made a nuisance of himself around women. At the time, Gallagher was unmarried, but there were several women in the household, including his mother, sister, and a teenaged servant named Maryann Murray. According to the *Saint John Daily Telegraph* of April 5, 1909: "He appeared to be somewhat of a misogynist and was quite intractable while men were absent, but became very meek upon the appearance of Mr. Gallagher." This behaviour might explain why, many years later, Dedier Comeau was reluctant to leave Jerome alone in the house with women.

By late 1862 the Gallagher family had had enough. They may have demanded the Overseers of the Poor find a new caretaker for their difficult house guest. The gentleman got together, perhaps with others in the community, to find a final solution to their Gamby problem. What transpired next is perhaps the most shadowy and ominous part of this entire tale.

Chapter 10

The Plot

Many writers have claimed there was a conspiracy of silence surrounding the mystery of Jerome. There was—but it was not Jerome's self-imposed silence. Instead, it was the silence of a small community that came to regret its actions. Apparently, the people of Chipman did not realize the dark nature of the bargain they struck in 1863, and may have only learned much later what danger they placed the frozen foreigner in.

After much deliberation, the Overseers of the Poor came to the conclusion that Gamby had to go. He was not a citizen of Chipman, and the taxpayers could not be expected to pay for the upkeep of this difficult man any longer. But they could not simply drag him to another county in New Brunswick and leave him there. The letters they had written asking for aid from the provincial government left a paper trail, and any investigation would show that the legless man had been cast out of Chipman. Gamby had to be removed from New Brunswick completely, so that he could not be traced back to their riverside community.

The committee was approached by a gentleman who offered to carry out the deed for the fee of five pounds, no questions asked. There was something sinister about the man's proposal, and after some thought, the authorities of Chipman passed on his offer. But their problem would not go away on its own, and they were forced to reconsider the plan.

By mid-1863 a deal was struck with a man named W. Colwell, who may have been the local tax collector, and was likely not a very popular person in the parish. The details of the arrangement are sketchy, but it appears that Colwell planned to escort Gamby downriver to Saint John. From there he said he would book Gamby passage on a ship for Liverpool, England. In Liverpool, he could contact the Italian consulate and arrange for passage home.

The Overseers may have convinced themselves they were doing Gamby a great service. After all, he stood a much better chance of returning to his home country if he were left in a major seaport; however, this plan placed very ambitious expectations on a legless man who was unable to communicate. It would have been next to impossible for Gamby to make the arrangements necessary to return to Italy, especially since he had no money. Besides, no one knew for sure if his home was Italy. The flimsy plan to send Gamby to the Italian authorities in Liverpool sounds more like a cover-up. The Overseers of the Poor in Chipman must have suspected that the tax collector never intended to make sure Gamby arrived in Liverpool, but only to see that he was put aboard a ship sailing away from New Brunswick.

The committee members must have hoped Gamby's relocation in the summer of 1863 would be the last they would ever hear of the matter; however, the transaction the committee negotiated to remove the foreigner did not sit well with some people in the village. Word of a shady deal got out when it was discovered the man was never sent to Liverpool. Rumours spread that the man was abandoned on a beach just down the coast in Maine.

The *Saint John Freeman* picked up on the story, and it was reprinted in the *Halifax Morning Chronicle* on September 19, 1863, just over a week after Jerome was discovered in Sandy Cove. The headline screamed "Savage Barbarity," and condemned those responsible for dumping the "poor miserable helpless creature" on a beach in Maine. If the legless man had not been discovered by some children, he surely would have died from exposure, and the charge against the Chipman authorities would have been murder. Despite the foreigner's survival, the article in the *Freeman* demanded someone be held responsible for the crime, stating that it would "be a shame to the Province if such inhuman wretches be suffered to go wholly unwhipt of justice."

How the story came to appear in the *Saint John Freeman* in 1863 in such great detail, accurate except for the assertion that Gamby washed ashore in Maine, is unknown. Perhaps an enterprising reporter hanging around the docks in Saint John overheard the Chipman tax collector booking passage for Gamby with a schooner captain. It is more likely that a disgruntled citizen of Chipman, unhappy with the way the Gamby affair was handled, tipped off the newspaper.

The article sparked a controversy in Chipman. At least one citizen was concerned that the entire parish might be branded as negligent, when it was the Overseers of the Poor who were solely responsible for "this barbarous conduct." In a letter to the editor of the *Saint John Freeman*, printed September 22, 1863, a Chipman "ratepayer" was quick to defend his fellow citizens: "I beg to assure you that [the citizens] are in no way responsible for so daring an outrage on humanity. The serious charge must be borne solely by the Commissioners of the Poor of the district, who arranged, as I am informed, with the tax-collector to bring the unfortunate man to the city for the purpose of getting rid of him." The letter writer admitted that the Overseers of the Poor may have been duped by the tax collector and led to believe Gamby was in good hands, but he did not believe that this absolved them of their guilt in the matter.

Less than a month went by before the newspaper again turned the heat up on those who arranged to expel Jerome. Over the previous weeks, newspapers outside of New Brunswick had picked up the story and there was growing concern the affair was tainting the reputation of the entire province. The October 17, 1863, edition of the *Morning Freeman* quoted at length a Halifax newspaper article that suggested that New Brunswick's reputation had indeed been damaged:

> Such an act of barbarity it is seldom our duty to record, and we hope that no stone will be left unturned to bring all parties implicated to speedy and retributive justice. The case demands immediate action of the government, in order that the Province may be fully exonerated from the stigma which must rest upon it by acts of a few in its midst.

The same article in the *Freeman* clarified that the Italian man was actually abandoned in Nova Scotia. It said that if he had been sent to Maine as was earlier believed, the Americans quickly turned around and sailed him across the Bay of Fundy to Nova Scotia.

In a letter to the editor in the same edition of the *Freeman*, likely from the same angry citizen who had written to the paper the month before, it was revealed that the seedy tax collector who engineered Gamby's disappearance had vanished. After executing the instructions of the Overseers of the Poor, Colwell the tax collector, fled.

The letter writer suggested Colwell had other dishonest dealings in the town, perhaps with the full knowledge and cooperation of the parish authorities: "I have heard that the said tax-gatherer was not sworn in, and that he collected 25 cents poll-tax, instead of 15, the amount assessed."

The newspapers and the public in New Brunswick were screaming for an investigation into the Gamby affair, yet, the government seemed to ignore the controversy. In the provincial capital, Lieutenant-Governor Arthur Hamilton-Gordon paid little attention to the antics of the backwoods village. The lieutenant-governor detested the petty, corrupt politics of colonial backwaters like New Brunswick. After all, Hamilton-Gordon was the son of a British prime minister and his ambitions were far too lofty to allow him to waste time on such matters. He was a busy man. In a few years he would be one of the architects of the Charlottetown Conference, which led to Confederation.

While the story was pursued by newspapers in Halifax and New Brunswick, remarkably word of the controversy apparently did not extend down the long, narrow spit of land that is Digby Neck. The people of Sandy Cove were evidently unaware of the connection between their mystery man and the poor fellow who was cast out of New Brunswick. These were the days before the railway reached the town of Digby, and mail was delivered by steamship. News may have travelled fast along Digby Neck, but it took a much slower route on the mainland. It took several weeks for the discovery in Sandy

Cove to reach the Halifax newspapers, and by then the connection between this legless castaway and events across the Bay of Fundy was either overlooked, ignored, or felt to be merely coincidental.

As for the local authorities in Chipman, while they didn't have blood on their hands, there was certainly dirt under their fingernails. It appears they offered little in the way of response to the charges. Neither, does it seem, did those responsible offer anything in the way of an apology, lest an apology be interpreted as an admission of guilt. Unless someone was prepared to come forward and make a specific, legal charge against the Overseers of the Poor or the tax collector, the case wouldn't appear in any court. With Gamby now outside of New Brunswick jurisdiction, the tax collector missing, and the Overseers keeping mum, the entire affair slowly faded from the headlines.

The Overseers of the Poor were so determined to put the issue behind them they even stalled in paying the Gallagher family money owed for keeping Gamby. Poor George Gallagher was forced to petition the local justice of the peace for payment after several requests to the Overseers fell on deaf ears.

In fairness to the people of Chipman, the events that led to Gamby's exile were orchestrated by a small cadre of people, and the actions of the Overseers of the Poor should not be used as an excuse to condemn an entire community. There was genuine outrage among the citizens of Chipman over the treatment of the injured foreigner. People did speak out against the injustice at the time and demanded an investigation. For their part, the gentlemen who made up the Overseers of the Poor were acting in the best interests of the taxpayers of their community. They were pushed to desperation by a burden they felt was forced upon them, and they made a decision they may have later regretted.

Chapter 11

The Ship

Despite all the evidence, and even after Senator G. G. King confirmed the story in the newspapers in 1905, Judge Savary still had his doubts about the connection between Gamby and Jerome. Over the years sparse details emerged that were difficult for researchers like Savary to corroborate. The judge continued to delve into the story whenever possible and spoke with anyone who ever had contact with Jerome.

In 1908, Savary was researching an update on the mystery for the *New York Herald* when he discovered the final piece of the puzzle that convinced him that Jerome and New Brunswick's Gamby were indeed the same person.

Savary contacted Angus M. Gidney, who was a young man of fourteen when Jerome came to stay with his family in Mink Cove. Angus's father, William, made every attempt to get Jerome to reveal his secrets, but gave up in frustration before sending the man to live with Jean Nicola in Meteghan. The lessons Angus learned during this time about caring for those less fortunate seemed to stay with him, and like other members of his family he took an active interest in politics and public affairs. Angus was elected to the provincial legislature as a Liberal in 1895 and served until 1910. When Nova Scotia's legislative assembly approved the weekly stipend for the family who cared for Jerome, Angus endorsed it with unique insight.

In a letter preserved among Savary's personal correspondence, Angus Gidney told the judge about a voyage his cousin, Samuel Gidney, took from Nova Scotia to Boston sometime around 1879. During the trip, the schooner Samuel was sailing on put in for the night at the port of Little River, Maine, and two local men came aboard for a chat. When the locals learned the schooner hailed from Sandy Cove, one man asked the sailors if they had ever heard of a legless man who was left on the beach in the area. Samuel Gidney, of course, replied yes. The man from Maine then confessed that he was among the crew who abandoned the legless man on the beach. He had been on a small boat fishing off the coast of New Brunswick when the crew was approached with the proposition of taking a legless man across the Bay of Fundy to Nova Scotia. They accepted ten dollars, took the human cargo, and set sail across the bay. Samuel Gidney himself wrote a short note to Judge Savary confirming this story, but was unable to provide any more details.

It seems remarkable that the members of the Gidney family kept this story to themselves until questioned by Judge Savary. But Samuel and Angus were busy people, entrepreneurs and business-men. In their practical world, they may have given little thought to Jerome once they knew he was safely being cared for among the Acadians. As an elected politician, Angus may have given priority to the concerns and issues of his constituents, and could not afford the time to follow up the case of an abandoned New Brunswicker. On the other hand, maybe they didn't want to spoil the mystery in which their family played a central role.

By the time Savary learned these new facts from Gidney, he still was convinced Jerome's amputations were fresh when he was dis-covered in Sandy Cove, which is why he was so reluctant to believe that Jerome and Gamby were the same person. According to the story Gidney told Savary, Gamby's legs were cut off in March. Savary assumed Gidney meant March 1863, the same year Jerome was found in Sandy Cove. This led Savary to incorrectly conclude that the operation was performed about five months before his dis-covery at Sandy Cove, which supported "the opinion of those who first saw him there that his legs had not been amputated more than six months."

The legend of Jerome being found with fresh amputations wrapped in bloody bandages is false; however, this incorrect assumption allowed Judge Savary to finally accept that Jerome came to Nova Scotia from New Brunswick. Armed with this new information from Samuel Gidney, Savary wrote directly to Senator G. G. King for more details in 1909, but did not receive an immediate reply. Savary felt that Senator King probably knew nothing more about the case, or did "not wish to expose too glaringly the disgraceful conduct of his old neighbors, the officers of the municipality who were guilty of such a base transaction."

Unfortunately, Samuel Gidney was unable to provide the name of the boat that ferried Jerome across the bay, or the identity of the captain. There was no indication that the small fishing boat was the mysterious Colombo that Jerome had mentioned when asked the name of his ship. The Colombo was more likely the name of the ship that brought Jerome over from Europe. By 1908, Judge Savary felt far too much time had passed to ever successfully track down Jerome's ship. The information he learned from Samuel Gidney was the closest the judge would come to finding the boat that once carried Jerome.

However, a mysterious painting hanging inside a small glass display case at the Maritime Museum of the Atlantic on the Halifax waterfront may offer a clue about the ship that brought Jerome to North America. The painting depicts the great freeze of 1859, an unusually harsh winter, when the normally unfrozen Halifax

Harbour was choked with ice. The watercolour shows the Cunard steamship RMS *America* entering Halifax Harbour on February 14, with cannon firing in salute to the lieutenant-governor.

In the background of the painting are several unidentified ships tied up at the wharf in the frozen harbour on the very day the RMS *America* triumphantly broke through the ice. One of these unremarkable transatlantic vessels was a brigantine that had arrived in Halifax from Great Britain, unloaded its cargo, and was likely waiting for the ice to break up. This ship was called *Columbus*. Aboard this icebound ship may have been the man who became famous as Jerome.

On Saturday, February 12, 1859, the people of Halifax woke up to another frigid day in what had become an almost unbearably cold winter. Those citizens who turned to the *Halifax Morning Chronicle* for the latest news found on the front page an advertisement by the James Scott company, a dealer in imported casks of wine, liquors, ports, and ales. The announcement read:

COLUMBUS
The undersigned has received per above vessel from
London—15
Hnds. Bass's India Pale Ale, October brewing—superior
to any in the market.
Will be ready for bottling in a very short time.

The *Columbus* had arrived in Halifax Harbour less than a month earlier, before the ice set in, on Tuesday, January 18, 1859.

A few months earlier on October 8, 1858, a ship called *Colombo* arrived in Gravesend, England, a port at the mouth of the Thames, and a few days later on October 22, a vessel the newspaper listed as *Columbu* was docked in London and preparing to leave for Halifax. While it is impossible to know for certain, it seems the name *Columbu* must have been a newspaper misprint, because on November 5, a ship named *Columbus* was listed as readying to leave London for Halifax. It arrived in Nova Scotia on January 18, 1859. This is the only ship found thus far that matches the name given by Jerome, and that sailed from Europe at the time when he is believed to have arrived in Canada.

The *Columbus* remained in port at Halifax until March 25, and then disappeared.

Given what we now know about Jerome's life before he appeared in Sandy Cove, it is entirely likely this ship left Halifax and headed for a port in northern New Brunswick. It is also possible that Jerome changed ships more than once. He may have sailed aboard the *Columbus* from Europe to Nova Scotia, where he jumped ship and either signed on, or stowed away on, another ship en route to New Brunswick.

Judge Savary was never able to find the legendary ship that brought Jerome across the Atlantic. Even though his meticulous research unveiled much about Jerome's origins, there were still many things the judge could not discover about the mystery man. With so much of the story left to be told, the judge's interest in Jerome lasted the rest of his life. His numerous letters to newspapers as far away as New York led people to view Judge Savary as an expert on the Jerome mystery. Nearly one hundred years later, Yarmouth historian Arthur Thurston wrote that Judge Savary's "voluminous writings reveal the whole story" of Jerome although the judge himself was somewhat more modest about his contributions to the legend.

The outgoing and eloquent Judge could not have been more different than the reclusive, silent Jerome, yet their lives were inextricably linked. Jerome detested and resented any meddling or intrusion into his silent world. However, the work of Judge Savary to uncover the stranger's true origin and identity may actually have been welcome by Jerome. If Jerome's secrets were revealed to all, he would have ceased to be an oddity that was probed and pestered by curiosity seekers. Quite simply, had Judge Savary succeeded in telling the world the truth about the mystery man, Jerome would have found the peace and privacy he so desperately wanted.

Chapter 12

The Voice

Throughout his life, Jerome was secretive, obstinate, and short-tempered. His odd behaviour helped fuel the years of wild speculation about his origins. Accepting that Jerome was injured and operated on in New Brunswick may help explain why he was so difficult.

The amputation of his legs must have been very traumatic; after all, it is likely that Jerome did not understand what was being done to him or why. While Dr. Peters was evidently a skillful physician, the language barrier and shock of Jerome's hypothermia made communicating with him nearly impossible. All he knew was that when he regained consciousness from the hazy ether-induced fog, both his legs had been stolen from him.

This event may have done more to shape Jerome's personality than any other. It is possible that the fear Jerome experienced on Dr. Peter's surgical table resulted in an intense phobia against being touched, or in his view, violated, that lasted the rest of his life. In later years Jerome reacted with revulsion and violence at any attempt to examine him. He also demonstrated a fear of doctors and medicine. Madeleine Genevieve, Jean Nicola's stepdaughter recalled that Jerome would only drink water, and was repulsed by medicine: "A doctor tried to give him whiskey to loosen his tongue, as they say, Gerome would not touch it, muttering a word which my father said meant medicine. And he was always afraid of medicine." Madeleine Genevieve and her family believed that Jerome's violent refusal of any medicine was an indication he had once been drugged against his will. In 1906 she told a New York newspaper reporter that when she was a young girl Jerome had revealed something to her about the loss of his legs: "Gerome had once told me his legs had been hurt by chains and that they had been cut off on a table."

Could it be that Jerome protested so vigorously while on Dr. Peter's operating table that the surgeon and his assistants had to secure the thrashing foreigner with chains? The abject horror he must have felt at being chained to a table, drugged into unconsciousness, and awakening to find himself mutilated is incomprehensible.

Dr. Augustus Robinson, a neighbour of Jean Nicola in Meteghan, recalled Jerome's stubborn reaction to physicians. Robinson began practicing medicine in Meteghan a year or so after Jerome came to live in the community. When he arrived in the area the locals were abuzz with talk and speculation about the legless stranger. Jerome is remembered as having been physically strong and generally in robust health for most of his life; however, there were rare times that he stopped eating, and the doctor was called to examine him. On one such occasion, Robinson tried to persuade the uncooperative Jerome to stick out his tongue with limited success. Robinson was quoted about his patient in the December 9, 1906, issue of the *New York Herald:* "I had to put my fingers on his chin, at the same time pressing it down to open his mouth, and thrusting my own tongue out. He would then do it in a faltering way."

While Jerome's amputation was a success from a strictly physical, surgical point of view, the operation may have caused some profound, permanent psychological damage. What emotions does someone experience when their legs are literally cut out from beneath them? Shock…fear…horror…rage? Jerome suffered from these devastating emotions in grim silence. That Jerome suffered is indisputable. His foul moods, anger, agitation, and depression are signs the poor soul experienced overwhelming personal anxiety.

He was known to lash out violently at anyone who pestered him. His frightful rages would last for days before he descended into a deep depression. At times he behaved as if he were besieged by some unspeakable inner torment—as if he were locked in a silent struggle with invisible demons.

Madeleine Genevieve Comeau described the silent anguish she had seen Jerome experience when she was a child: "When he thought he was alone, I saw him hold his face in his hands as if he were suffering and then tear his hair. Another time I saw him put his hand on a red hot stove. It never occurred to me that he was torturing himself as expiation for his sins; but one hears of such things."

Jerome spent most of his time huddled near the kitchen stove. This was his comfort zone, a place where he felt safe, so it seems unlikely that he placed his hand on the hot metal by accident. Could he have intentionally burned himself as some sort of penance? Self-flagellation and mortification of the flesh are known practices among some Christians seeking spiritual cleansing for personal sins. Still others view mortification of the flesh as a way to share in the pain suffered by Christ on the cross. There is evidence Jerome was a Roman Catholic. He was seen to pray and make the sign of the cross, although he refused the rosary when offered one. Just how deep Jerome's religious convictions ran is almost impossible to guess.

Burning himself or tearing out his own hair may have been Jerome's sad way of doing penance, but it may also have been a diversionary tactic used to distract himself from some personal pain he was unable to articulate. Maybe something unbearable was going on inside his head that only a greater, physical pain could counteract.

Jerome's struggle with his inner demons is indisputable. It is possible that his demons took the form of phantoms, the common phenomenon suffered by amputees who continue to feel their missing limb long after it has been cut off. Being haunted by the ghost of a missing limb can be frightening, especially if the amputee does not understand what is happening or why. An amputee may feel an overwhelming itch on the bottom of a missing foot, an itch that is impossible to scratch. Cramps or spasms in a leg that is no longer there may cause the sufferer to doubt his own sanity.

While phantom pain is fairly common, it is not very well understood. Unfortunately Jerome did not have the therapeutic benefit of being able to discuss the torment of phantom pain in his absent legs. It is also unlikely that Jerome's surgeon or any of his caregivers would have been capable of explaining that such phantom feelings were normal. In the early 1860s, the first real research into the impact of amputations was just getting underway in the United States among the countless soldiers who lost limbs during the American Civil War.

Jerome could not describe the abyss that engulfed him. He could not understand it, ask questions, or seek help to escape from it. It is little wonder the poor soul was sullen and prone to violent outbursts. Given his obvious and apparent torment, why did Jerome not speak out? What was the secret of Jerome's silence?

The legend of the injured castaway inexplicably abandoned on a remote beach was so compelling because despite the combined, intense efforts of countless people who tried to coax him to speak, he never told his rescuers who he was, where he came from, or why his legs were cut away. Most written accounts of the story claim that except for mumbling something sounding like Jerome, he never spoke at all, which led some people to believe Jerome refused to talk because he was under a pledge of silence or secrecy.

The belief that Jerome was only capable of growling and mumbling led to some other fantastic theories about his lack of a voice. In his book *Sagas of the Land and Sea*, master storyteller and author Roland Sherwood wrote about rumours Jerome's palate had been deliberately cut to keep him from speaking. It is difficult to comprehend why someone would try to ensure Jerome's silence by such a complicated surgery. Cutting his tongue out completely would have been an easier and more reliable way to keep him quiet, so it is no surprise this theory has also been put forward. However, Dr. Augustus Robinson examined Jerome and managed with some difficulty to get him to stick out his tongue, proving his lack of a voice was not due to lack of a tongue.

Along with his tongue and palate, Jerome's vocal cords were also targeted by conspiracy theorists fishing for a physical reason for his silence. Among the fascinating characters in the charming novel *Fog Magic* by Julia Sauer is a pitiful soul called Anthony who was based on Jerome. In the novel, foreign sailors who visit the fogbound village are brought before the legless Anthony to try to converse with him in a variety of languages. Greta, the inquisitive young heroine of the story, is told some villagers believe that whoever cut off Anthony's legs "cut the vocal cords in his throat too, so he never could speak—and maybe tell something they didn't want known."

Despite the enduring legends of his silence, the truth is Jerome wasn't silent at all. He spoke clearly on several occasions, while at other times he struggled to speak and seemed frustrated at his own failed attempts. When he actually blurted out a word or two, Jerome himself was taken by surprise. After many years, it seems he gave up trying to speak and was reduced to growling like an animal, but sometimes late at night, when he believed he was alone, Jerome could be heard singing in a beautiful voice in some foreign language.

Some writers referred to Jerome as feeble-minded or of a disordered mind, and one even compared him to a dumb animal. The late Yarmouth historian Arthur Thurston felt that, "in all probability he was defective of speech, and being illiterate as well, there was no way he was able to communicate." Other accounts state matter-of-factly that Jerome didn't talk because he was a mute. The headline of a story in the *Halifax Herald* on Tuesday, November 15, 1898, declared that Jerome was "Without a Name and Dumb for Forty Years." The article went on to further disrespect Jerome by calling him a halfwit. These words were attributed to then Nova

Scotia Premier George H. Murray, who told the paper "that he had seen this 'Jerome' during the past summer, and that the man is doubtless half-witted."

Some earlier writers simply stated the shock of his amputations so befuddled his mind that he was rendered incapable of speech. In a letter to the *Saint John Daily Telegraph* in 1909, Judge Savary wrote that the incredible trauma suffered by Jerome caused him to lose his mind. Savary inferred:

> That from the shock to his constitution by the amputation and exposure, he was becoming, but was not yet wholly demented, and it may well be that his being placed among French speaking people after he had learned a little English, accelerated the speechlessness into which his insanity developed.

The symptoms of his silence seem much more complicated than the many theories can account for. His silence cannot be easily explained away as just a result of shock from falling into a frozen river or the surgery that cost him his legs. His behaviour following his plunge into the icy river in 1859, and his obvious difficulties communicating with others seem to indicate he suffered some form of neurological damage.

Modern medical science may have finally provided an answer to the mystery of the voice of Jerome. The facts indicate that the behaviour displayed by Jerome when he tried to speak was the result of a stroke-induced aphasia. It remains impossible to prove for certain, but there were a number of conditions present that could have led Jerome to suffer a stroke, or perhaps a series of strokes.

A stroke, or brain attack, is caused when brain cells are damaged because of disruption of blood flow to the brain. The damage is the result of a lack of oxygen in the brain cells and can be caused by a blood clot or bleeding in the brain. It is well known today that strokes are one of the leading causes of neurologic, or brain, damage; however, in the early 1860s, the medical research linking strokes, brain damage, and communication disorders was only in its infancy.

There are several events leading up to and including Jerome's amputation that may have contributed to a stroke. The winter of 1859 was frigid, and Jerome may have been confused as a result of hypothermia as he wandered through the New Brunswick woods. After falling into the freezing river, and possibly hitting his head on a log, the debilitating effects of hypothermia seized Jerome even more quickly. The symptoms of hypothermia include slow and clumsy movements, confusion, and a drop in blood pressure. A sudden and prolonged drop in blood pressure is one cause of ischemic stroke, a disruption of blood flow to the brain.

Rescuing someone suffering from hypothermia is a delicate procedure. A victim of severe hypothermia may be mistaken for dead as his pulse plunges and heart rate drops to near zero. According to the *Merck Manual of Medical Information*, the victim must be handled gently and carefully since a sudden jolt can cause an irregular heartbeat or arrhythmia. The Conroy brothers who discovered the nearly frozen Jerome on the brow of logs were rough woodsmen, and it is unlikely they would have handled him with kid gloves. Despite their good intentions, the Conroys jostling may have caused Jerome to gain an abnormal heart rhythm. This is a common precursor to an embolic stroke, which occurs when the abnormal heartbeat dislodges a clot into the bloodstream. If Jerome experienced a stroke because of a blood clot caused by an irregular heartbeat, there is a good chance he suffered more than one stroke, as the danger of stroke does not pass until the irregular heartbeat is corrected.

The next event that may have caused Jerome to have a stroke was the administration of anesthesia before his surgery. It is impossible to know for certain if Jerome was knocked out prior to his amputation. The use of anesthetic was still novel in 1859, but even today, nearly 150 years later, it poses many risks to the patient. It is not unheard of for a patient under anesthesia to experience a quick and dangerous drop in blood pressure. As mentioned above, someone with severely low blood pressure is in danger of suffering a massive stroke.

Finally, the surgery itself may have caused Jerome to have a stroke. Heavy blood loss can lead to a drop in blood pressure and stroke. While Jerome's amputations were performed by a skillful surgeon, there was still the possibility of complications and infections—especially since it was still a few years before Lister's innovations in antiseptic surgical practices were widely used. The formation of a clot as the result of the surgery, or from complications following his amputations, while fairly uncommon today, cannot be discounted.

The myths and misconceptions about Jerome's behaviour and speech emerged because, at the time of his discovery on the Sandy Cove beach in 1863, few people suspected there was a link between strokes, brain damage, and communication disorders. At the same time, across the ocean in France, physician Paul Broca (1824–1880) was pioneering scientific research into how different functions, such as speech, are located in certain areas of the brain. In 1861, Broca discovered that difficulties with speech and communication were often found in people who suffered damage to an area in the left hemisphere of the brain, now known as Broca's area. Broca's work confirmed that the impact of a stroke on speech and communication depends on what area of the brain is damaged. The resulting speech disorder, known as aphasia, comes in several different forms and varies widely in severity and symptoms.

Jerome was capable of speaking, but usually only one or two words at a time. Those who heard him talk reported that he uttered words "as if he had forgotten himself," or when he was taken by surprise. At other times he struggled to make himself understood and became easily frustrated and angry, emitting only growls or grunts. "He would get mad when he wanted things, because he wouldn't ask for them," recalled Madeleine Genevieve.

Jerome's agitation when trying to speak even a single word is consistent with a specific form of aphasia called expressive aphasia or Broca's aphasia. This form of aphasia was present in Broca's most famous patient and test subject, who was named Tan because it was the only word he could say. The parallels with Jerome are obvious, since he got his name the same way.

Unlike some forms of brain damage where the sufferer is not aware of their limitations, a person with Broca's aphasia realizes he has a problem. This awareness usually results in extreme frustration, and leads to violent outbursts and deep depression.

Jerome would fly into fearful fits of rage and become very agitated when pressured to speak or answer questions. He would also descend into a terribly foul mood after accidentally, or absent-mindedly saying a word or two. But Jerome spoke quite freely and easily when he was calm, peaceful, and amused. Again, this behaviour is consistent with Broca's aphasia. A syndrome called apraxia of speech, the physical inability to form words despite great effort to do so, often accompanies this type of aphasia. The more a sufferer tries to speak, the more difficulty they have, yet automatic, almost spontaneous speech occurs when they are not trying. This can happen when there is no pressure to speak, like it did when Jerome was in the company of happy children at play.

There may have been something else about playing children that appealed to Jerome. The simple, repetitive, rhyming nursery songs of youngsters have a special appeal for aphasics. In a remarkable phenomenon, many aphasic patients who have lost the ability to speak even simple words are still able to sing. According to neurologist Dr. Oliver Sacks, musical ability is so deeply embedded in our neural wiring that it can somehow survive even the most extensive brain damage. In his book *Musicophilia,* Dr. Sacks describes a stroke patient incapable of uttering a single word whose caregivers later overhear him belting out loudly and clearly an old show tune. Singing and music therapies are now common treatments for aphasia patients as it is believed to help make the necessary neural connections to compensate for damage to the language areas of the brain. It is a shame that when Jerome was overheard singing late at night, someone did not attempt to join him in song, or introduce more music into his daily life, as this may have been the key to breaking through his wall of silence.

Other aspects of Jerome's character are better understood when the possibility of aphasia is introduced. At times Jerome seemed paranoid, distrustful, and fearful around adults, especially strangers. Many of these strangers were part of the constant parade of visitors who appeared before Jerome to pester him in foreign languages or to stare at him as an entertaining curiosity. When they spoke to him, they lacked sincerity, compassion, and caring. The tone of their voices may have been condescending and artificial.

Along with trouble speaking, some people with aphasia have difficulty comprehending or understanding words. While they may not grasp the meaning of individual words, they are still very sensitive to the tone and inflection of speech, and are keenly tuned in to the feelings behind the words. Dr. Sacks declared that it is impossible to lie to an aphasia patient. Like dogs that are used to sniff out falsehood, Dr. Sacks believes aphasics have a deep sense of who can and can't be trusted. Jerome may have known who had his best interests at heart, and reacted with fear and violence towards those who wished to exploit him.

Unfortunately, those people who truly wanted to help Jerome regain his lost voice did not have the ability to do so. Only now, nearly 150 years later, are we able to understand Jerome's silence was not the result of a stubborn refusal to speak, although he was indeed stubborn. Nor can his silence be explained as simple ignorance of the language spoken by his caregivers, although he was evidently an Italian among primarily French-speaking people. His silence was not as simple as that. All clues point to Jerome being afflicted with some form of aphasia. Since aphasia is commonly caused by stroke, it is difficult not to conclude that Jerome was the unfortunate victim of a terrible one-two punch that robbed him of his voice. It is practically unheard of for people afflicted with severe aphasia to spontaneously begin speaking normally again without help.

As the years passed and Jerome got older, many hoped that he would finally speak and reveal his secrets. The legends say that as he approached death Jerome tried to talk more frequently, but was no longer physically able. Many writers shared the view expressed by Lilah Bird Smith in *The Nova Scotia Historical Quarterly* that, "in later years his long silence seemed to have resulted in the atrophy of his vocal chords, for although he seemed willing to break his long silence, the power to do so seemed to be gone."

Again, these past chroniclers of Jerome's story have it wrong. It is very unlikely that vocal cords would atrophy, or become stiff from non-use. The vocal cords are muscles used for many things besides speaking words, like coughing and throat clearing. Jerome was known to frequently make growling and grumbling noises that vigorously exercised his vocal cords.

His growling, grumbling, and generally foul moods are telling signs of the depression that gripped Jerome. Again, depression is common among stroke victims and those with aphasia. Unable to communicate, aphasia patients can become socially isolated and withdrawn, as Jerome did, leading to even deeper depression.

Jerome knew he could not speak, but he did not know why. And no one else knew why either. Symptoms of aphasia can be mis-understood as a mental impairment. A doctor commenting in the 1930s remembered Jerome by saying: "He was an idle man with an idle mind."

Mercifully, Jerome did emerge from his depression on occasion. When he was among children his veil of silence was sometimes lifted, and Jerome was able to express himself. Free from the expectations and constant questions of the adult world, Jerome was allowed to, briefly, find his voice again. Some say Jerome tried to speak as he approached death, but he continued to frustrate those who hoped he would reveal his secrets.

Chapter 13

The Legacy

Jerome, the man who spent his life shunning attention, found the perfect time to die in obscurity. He passed away quietly on April 15, 1912, a date since immortalized as the day the *Titanic* sank. The silent man who grabbed headlines around the globe died while the world waited for news of survivors from the North Atlantic. Despite the international attention focused on the *Titanic*, Jerome's death still managed to make page four of the April 20, 1912, edition of the *Halifax Morning Chronicle*, proving that the anonymous man's fame was still considerable.

While the entire world shared in the grief of the unimaginable tragedy at sea, an elderly woman mourned with her family over the loss of Jerome. Zabeth Comeau had anticipated Jerome's death. He had been ill for three weeks before he died. His coughing and wheezing, so strange for a man always in robust health, indicated a chest infection such as bronchitis.

Zabeth had her son fetch Father Alphonse Benoit Côté, Meteghan's parish priest. While it was generally believed Jerome was a Roman Catholic, Zabeth refused to allow the man to die without taking steps to guarantee his immortal soul was protected. Father Côté baptized the dying man before anointing him with the sacred oils of extreme unction—the blessed sacrament of the last rites.

As is customary with the last rites, Father Côté would have offered to hear Jerome's dying confession. Between fits of coughing, it is believed he tried to speak, but in these final moments, Father Côté learned nothing. Whatever sins or secrets Jerome held silently within his heart were forgiven by the priest.

After his death, Jerome's body was sent by wagon down the road to the cemetery next to the Meteghan church. He was buried in the section of the cemetery reserved for unbaptized babies. A large number of people gathered around his burial plot to witness the final journey of this famous man. A simple wooden marker was stuck into the earth over his grave. The damp fog and salty sea air, so common in this coastal community, quickly ate away at Jerome's grave marker. Within a few years the wood rotted and became one with the soil. With the disappearance of any sign to mark the exact location of his grave, the man who hated to be molested and bothered finally had the privacy he so desperately craved.

His obituary in the *Halifax Morning Chronicle* did little to dispel the myths and legends surrounding the man, and in fact contained a number of errors that were repeated by later writers. The article began simply, but dramatically: "Jerome died this morning (April 19), his secret dying with him. The sentence seems but an unimportant piece of news, but there is a great mystery of international importance surrounding this man, who was believed by many to be a son of a nobleman of some foreign nation."

The obituary incorrectly stated Jerome died on April 19, when in fact it was four days earlier. It also mistakenly claimed he was abandoned in Sandy Cove in 1854, nine years too early, and said the person who discovered him on the beach was Samuel Gidney, robbing George "Collie" Albright of his rightful place in the saga.

Jerome's obituary mentioned, but dismissed his New Brunswick connection, instead reporting that the story of Jerome being injured, then cast out of the province was "very much doubted by the older inhabitants who first saw him." It dismissed the possibility of discovering the truth, stating "the people in this vicinity have given up the solving of the great mystery that closed today in death, thus ending one of the greatest secrets that ever occurred on this continent."

Despite all the evidence that proved that Jerome was indeed the frozen man found in the New Brunswick woods, the people of Nova Scotia would not give up their mystery man so easily. As Jerome's obituary showed, there was an almost desperate desire to not just cling to the mystery, but preserve, protect, and perpetuate it. Perhaps this is the reason Judge Savary's research and evidence of Jerome's connection to New Brunswick were forgotten by the time Jerome died.

For thirty years following his death, the tale of Jerome seemed to die too. With the passing of the main character, newspapers were no longer interested in revisiting the story. But it wasn't a newspaper that revived the legend for a new generation of mystery-lovers. Jerome's story gained new life on the radio.

In the early 1940s radios in homes across Halifax crackled and hissed as listeners tuned their sets to CHNS to catch the popular program *Tales Told Under the Old Town Clock,* hosted by Colonel William C. Borrett. Families rushed home from church on Sunday to catch the show at 12:45. During the program Colonel Borrett regaled listeners with odd tales, mysteries, and legends drawn from his encyclopedic knowledge of Nova Scotia history and folklore.

During one of his popular fifteen-minute broadcasts in 1942 Colonel Borrett brought the mystery of Jerome back into the homes of thousands of Nova Scotians.

With pipe in hand and in his distinctive radio voice, Borrett would often instruct his listeners to fetch their maps and follow along as he took his audience on a journey down the dusty back roads of Nova Scotia history. Borrett travelled frequently for business, and during this broadcast in 1942 he told his listeners about a train trip he had taken from Yarmouth on the Dominion Atlantic Railway. His seatmate for the journey was a Mr. F. G. J. Comeau, who was general freight and passenger agent for the railway. The pair shared an interest in Nova Scotia history and they chatted about local folklore to pass the time. As the train approached Digby, Mr. Comeau casually asked Borrett, "Did you ever hear the story of Jerome?"

By the time of Colonel Borrett's rail journey few people outside of the French Acadian region of Clare remembered Jerome's story, and Borrett admitted he had never even heard of the man. Always eager to learn a new story for his radio program, Borrett immediately sat up and took notice. Comeau then revealed for the colonel what has become the best-known version of Jerome's legend. All the elements were included in the radio broadcast—the strange, anonymous ship; Jerome's freshly amputated legs protruding from expensive European clothing; the singular utterances of the words *Jerome*, *Colombo*, and *Trieste*; and the fantastic theories about pirate mutinies and secret societies.

It was a ripping good yarn told with all the flair of a master storyteller. Borrett's audience loved it. He later claimed "that the story of Jerome was considered by many of [his listeners] among the most interesting of the Town Clock series of tales." As it turns out, the fellow who told the story, F. G. J. Comeau, had more than a passing interest in Jerome, and had written about the mystery himself.

Jerome's story gained even more renown in late 1942 when Borrett's program was spun off into a series of successful books. The first book in the series reached an even wider audience than the radio show, and Borrett received numerous letters from readers anxious to learn more about the fascinating tale of Jerome. Other letter writers offered more information on the story and some compelling clues in the Jerome mystery.

Not long after Borrett aired the story, he was contacted by a woman named Margaret Ells, an employee of the Nova Scotia Archives in Halifax. Ms. Ells had uncovered an old, yellowed newspaper clipping she felt would be of interest to the radio broadcaster. Indeed, the newspaper clipping provided new insight into the origins of Jerome.

The newspaper clipping that was brought to Colonel Borrett's attention was likely from 1905, when there was a flurry of renewed media interest in the Jerome story. It may have contained the letter to the editor by Mr. C. O. Foss. With this clipping, the weave of the tightly spun mystery began to unravel once again.

Colonel Borrett himself played a part in maintaining the mystery of Jerome, even though he had all the evidence in his possession. In a follow-up radio broadcast, and in a sequel to his popular book, *Tales Told Under the Old Town Clock,* in 1945, Borrett revealed the evidence linking Jerome to Gamby in New Brunswick. Other books based on his radio show followed, with a collection of the most popular stories reprinted in the 1950s. Oddly, in this compendium, Borrett's original mystery story about Jerome was reprinted, instead of the updated version from 1945 featuring the New Brunswick evidence.

One year after Borrett's original broadcast in 1942, the popular myth of Jerome was featured in Julia L. Sauer's award-winning novel *Fog Magic,* a book that is beloved on Digby Neck. The novel is a delightful fable about a disappearing way of life, and the magical fog that transports a young girl to a small village lost in time. Sauer was an American who fell in love with Digby Neck while on vacation in the 1930s. Over tea in local homes Julia absorbed the rich history and folklore of the area and learned of the fascinating characters that once walked the shores of Digby Neck. Many of these characters appeared in *Fog Magic,* but often with different names.

In the novel, Jerome appears as a deaf, dumb, and legless seaman known only as Anthony who was discovered on the beach. Anthony spends his days sitting with his back against a picket fence, acting as a babysitter for small children. He peers through the fence pickets—like the bars of a symbolic prison—staring at strangers passing by. Greta, the spirited young heroine of the novel, begs her friend Retha's mother to tell her theory about the mysterious Anthony:

I don't know, child. In my day I've believed one thing after another. But no theory holds water. Except," She paused for a minute and then went on slowly, "I can never believe that Anthony is simple. There's a brain and intelligence at work behind those fine eyes. I've always believed he could hear too, but Retha's father laughs at me. No, Anthony's helpless but he's not hopeless. And he's looking for someone, I'll be bound. Whether it's friend or foe, I don't presume to guess. You've noticed how long he looks at every stranger? Well, some day I'm hoping Anthony finds the face he is looking for.

When a foreign sailor arrives one day, the villagers are more relieved than disappointed that the man is unable to communicate with the silent Anthony. It seems author Julia Sauer was commenting on how the villagers didn't really want to know the truth about Anthony. They cherished their mystery man and preferred him to remain just that—mysterious.

The characters in *Fog Magic* are not the only people who preferred mystery over the mundane truth. By the late 1940s, Jerome was generating regular headlines once again. Not since before his death had he attracted so much attention. But in the dozens of newspaper and magazine reports about Jerome in the mid-twentieth century, the New Brunswick affair was referred to only in passing. Answers to the questions around his sudden appearance on Digby Neck were forgotten or ignored, and the tale reverted back to a classic mystery story. Along with newspaper headlines, Jerome became a regular feature in books on Nova Scotia history, folklore, and in the emerging travel and tourism industry. Jerome certainly attracted plenty of visitors when he was alive, and travel writers began to recognize his value as a tourist attraction long after he passed away.

One of the first such travel books was *Down in Nova Scotia: My Own, My Native Land*, by Clara Dennis (1881–1958), daughter of *Halifax Herald* newspaper magnate Senator William Dennis. In 1950, Nova Scotian historian, author, and tourism promoter Will R. Bird wrote his own travelogue, *This is Nova Scotia*. Bird describes a conversation with a senior citizen in Clare who offered the story of Jerome. After telling the tale, the man concluded: "One great, very great mystery," adding, "he could have been a prince, a robber, who know[s]? One guess is as good as any other." As Bird discovered, it wasn't just the travel writers who recognized the value of Jerome. The locals were starting to play along and promote the mystery themselves, often with a sly wink.

As Jerome was increasingly mentioned in Nova Scotia tourism literature, he was also growing more mythical. Few newspaper articles offered any new facts about the story, and some shamelessly copied entire paragraphs from previous articles, which is especially unfortunate since many earlier stories contained incorrect information.

One person who added more to Jerome's story was prolific writer and historian Robert Blauveldt (1894–1975). In 1966, in a supplement to the *Yarmouth Vanguard* called "Jerome—The 'Mystery Man' of Clare," Blauveldt described how difficult it was to locate anyone in the district of Clare who could tell him anything about Jerome. Blauveldt wrote that "many years had passed, and very few people in the district even remembered the old man, so not much was learned."

Robert Blauveldt's claim that he could not find anyone who remembered Jerome is difficult to understand considering the significant role his story plays in the mythology of the French Shore of Clare. The Acadians of this region have always been adept storytellers and it is hard to believe Blauveldt's search for someone to interview was unsuccessful. After all, descendents of Zabeth and Dedier Comeau still live in Saint Alphonse to this day, and many of them remember fondly the stories they were told of Jerome from their older relatives.

One possible explanation for his failure to find someone to speak with is that the Acadians were suspicious of his motives. Ever since the American Henry Wadsworth Longfellow wrote *Evangeline* in 1847, many Acadians have felt they had to suffer the surrender of their stories to non-Acadian writers, and have been rightfully protective of them.

Acadian history from the expulsion on is essentially an oral history, passed down through generations of storytellers. In the late 1960s, Acadian culture and heritage experienced a revival. In order to preserve their fragile oral history, tape recordings were made of many older Acadians telling the stories and traditions of their people. Many of these tape recordings are preserved in the archives of

Université Sainte-Anne in Church Point, Nova Scotia, and a number of them contain references to the famous mystery man.

Jerome's story benefitted from this emerging interest in Acadian heritage, as it allowed people to view his story through a new lens. For the first time, the societal and cultural context in which Jerome lived was explored from a uniquely Acadian viewpoint. Jerome did not just live with the Comeau family for many years, but was a member of a close-knit community with a rich history. Popular writer, historian, and Order of Canada recipient J. Alphonse Deveau (1918–2004) wrote about Jerome on several occasions and brought his unique Acadian perspective to the story.

The role of the family in Acadian culture, particularly the matriarch or mother of the family, was the focus of Edith Comeau-Tufts's (another member of the Order of Canada) version of the Jerome story. Her 1977 book *Acadienne de Clare* tells the stories of a number of remarkable Acadian women. Comeau-Tufts comments that in the celebrated story of Jerome, the central figure of Elizabeth "Zabeth" Comeau is often ignored. As an Acadian wife and mother, Zabeth worked tirelessly and selflessly to raise a large Catholic family with the added burden of a difficult, ungrateful celebrity house guest. If there is a candidate for sainthood among the characters of the Jerome story, the resilient Zabeth Comeau would certainly qualify.

Appreciating the central role of the family in Acadian culture is key to understanding how Jerome's memory is preserved and protected in Clare today. While Jerome was not an Acadian, he was considered part of the family—not just the Comeau family, but the larger community. Jerome is written about fondly in the personal family histories of many people in Clare. Zabeth and Dedier's great-granddaughter, Eva Boudreau, and her sisters, have spent years compiling the Comeau family history with a chapter devoted to Jerome. Like the work of many amateur historians and genealogists, the history of Eva Boudreau's family is something to be shared only among family members, and not intended for publication.

In the 1970s Jerome entered onto the dramatic stage for the first time. Acadian playwright, author, and educator Germaine Comeau wrote the acclaimed play *The Return of Jerome*, which was staged in 1976, and later adapted for radio, winning a Radio-Canada prize in 1987. In 1994, filmmaker and television director Phil Comeau brought Jerome to the big screen. The first true Acadian feature film, *Le Secret de Jérôme* is less about the silent title character than the rigid cultural norms and expectations of a small Acadian community in the mid-nineteenth century. The film was a huge hit in French-speaking Canada, especially in southwestern Nova Scotia and won several international awards, proving the story of Jerome still had the power to fascinate people around the world.

The success of the film again revived interest in the mystery and resurrected plans to erect a monument to Jerome in Meteghan. For years there were grumblings in the Clare community that it was unacceptable that the precise location of Jerome's gravesite was lost. On August 15, 2000, a stone grave marker bearing the name Jérôme was unveiled in the Meteghan parish cemetery. Sponsored by La Société Historique Acadienne de la Baie Ste. Marie, the marker is accompanied by an interpretive sign featuring a rare photo of Jerome, and a short history of his story in both French and English.

Jerome-mania struck again in 2007 in a way the attention-shunning man never could have imagined or tolerated. On April 15, 2007, the ninety-fifth anniversary of his death, a comprehensive, publicly-funded website about Jerome was officially launched in front of a large crowd at the École secondaire de Clare (Clare High School). The launch was a true community event, with many descendents of Zabeth and Dedier Comeau in attendance. The website is part of the Great Unsolved Mysteries in Canadian History project, which tackles several mysteries, including *Jerome: The Mystery Man of Baie Sainte-Marie.* The website makes available in one place much of the documented material on Jerome from the Nova Scotia Public Archives, the New Brunswick Provincial Archives, and the Centre Acadien at the Université Sainte-Anne.

The website itself almost took a backseat during the event. In traditional Acadian fashion, the evening included art, music, and even a little theatre. During the night, Meteghan artist Nora Robicheau unveiled her colourful painting of Jerome's story, depicting many of the major events of the man's life. Another highlight was the live debut—in both French and English—of a song about Jerome called "Fallen Angels" by musician Patrice Boulianne, founder of the East Coast Music Award-winning francophone band Blou.

The website launch followed a day of activities devoted to Jerome, including a mass in his honour at the Saint Alphonse church, and a special rededication of the Jerome monument in the Meteghan cemetery. When the interpretive sign next to the monument was erected in 2000, it had incorrectly stated he died on August 19, 1912. The Jerome monument had to be updated after his original death certificate was dusted off by website researchers Lise Robichaud and Caroline-Isabelle Caron of Queen's University.

Jerome returned to the stage in 2008, when The Two Planks and a Passion theatre company staged a drama based on his story in Canning, Nova Scotia. *Jerome: The Historical Spectacle*, by award-winning writer Ami McKay, explores how the appearance of Jerome brings out the best and worst in some members of a small community.

Over the last century, Jerome's story has been featured in literature, poems, and songs, and on stage, radio, the silver screen, and even the Internet. He continues to appear in tourism guides, books about Maritime mysteries and, oddly enough, books on ghosts and the paranormal. Jerome's legend evolved from a pure mystery story, to a tale of social injustice, to the subject of school history projects. But perhaps Jerome is most widely accepted today as a symbol of Acadian charity. When Jerome appeared in 1863, only a few generations had passed since the cruel expulsion of the Acadians from

Nova Scotia. It was a time when the francophone citizens of Clare had every reason to be suspicious of strangers who appeared on their shores. Yet Jerome was taken in, cared for, and considered a member of the family within a close-knit community. Despite being a difficult and ungrateful guest, Jerome was still treated tenderly, washed, clothed, and fed. It is no surprise that when a residential home for people with special needs was opened in 1989 in Church Point, it was named Maison Jerome.

Even with all the latest evidence scoured from provincial archives in Nova Scotia and New Brunswick, and information tucked away in personal family histories, there is still plenty of mystery left in Jerome's story. Next to nothing is known about how or why Jerome came to North America, or his life prior to plunging into the icy river in New Brunswick. Although it is generally accepted by most researchers today that Jerome came from Trieste in northern Italy, this is not known for certain. At one time or another, Jerome was said to have come from Spain, Ireland, the United States, Poland, England, Sri Lanka, Portugal, and a host of other countries. The issue of Jerome's hometown has never been definitively settled.

Jerome remains an enigma, with many unanswered questions about where he originally came from, why he abandoned ship in New Brunswick, and what brought him to Canada in the first place. But the greatest mystery of all is the mystery itself. Why do people still care about the mystery of Jerome nearly a century after his death?

Perhaps it is because the world still needs mystery men. A man without a past is a blank canvas upon which any of our hopes or expectations can be splashed.

While it was believed by many that Jerome was royalty, or perhaps a romantic pirate, today a mystery man is more likely to take the form of a tortured genius. Only a superior mind of exceptional intellectual or artistic ability would seek anonymity to escape from a world that insists on immediate information on everything and everyone.

Jerome, and all of history's mystery men share a similar reputation. People are willing, even eager to believe they are somehow more special, more gifted, and perhaps more worthy of wonder, contemplation, and pity. We are prepared to overlook and ignore evidence that might somehow show them to be just like everyone else. In Jerome's case, evidence of his true identity has been ignored and dismissed for over one hundred years.

In a community where the citizens are famous for telling stories, singing, and making music, the most famous resident of all was silent. While the whole world was fascinated by Jerome at times, he neither sought, nor enjoyed his fame. His mind caged in a legless body, trapped in a wordless world, he preferred only to be left alone, huddled close to a hot wood stove. When he dared to peek out from his hiding place, he was too often confronted with glaring faces and endless questions—questions Jerome refused to acknowledge.

Despite the evidence that clearly demonstrates the circumstances of Jerome's abandonment, Jerome's story has endured because it is more than just a mystery. If it were, we would cease to be interested once the mystery was revealed. Instead, we continue to care about Jerome because his is a human story. It is a story about caring, compassion, wonder, and adventure. Without doubt, it is a story that will continue to be told, explored, and debated for at least another hundred years.

Sources

Baigent, Michael, and Henry Lincoln and Richard Leigh. *Holy Blood, Holy Grail*. New York: Dell, 1983.

Baird, Rev. Frank. *History of the Parish of Chipman*. Sackville: Tribune Press, 1946.

Bird, Will R. *This Is Nova Scotia*. Toronto: The Ryerson Press, 1950.

Borrett, William C. *Tales Told Under the Old Town Clock*. Halifax: Imperial Publishing Company Ltd., 1942.

Borrett, William C. *Down East: Another Cargo of Tales Told Under the Old Town Clock*. Halifax: Imperial Publishing Ltd., 1945.

Bradley, Michael, with Deanna Theilmann-Bean. *Holy Grail Across the Atlantic: The Secret History of Canadian Discovery and Exploration*. Ontario: Hounslow Press, 1988.

Brown, George S. *Yarmouth Nova Scotia: A Sequel to Campbell's History.* Boston: Rand Avery Company Printers, 1888.

Bull, Mary Kate. *Sandy Cove.* Hantsport: Lancelot Press, 1978.

Carrington, Dorothy. *Corsica: Portrait of a Granite Island.* New York: The John Day Company, 1974.

Comeau-Tufts, Edith. *Acadienne de Clare.* Saulnierville: 1977.

Crooker, William S. *Tracking Treasure: In Search of East Coast Bounty.* Halifax: Nimbus Publishing, 1998.

Dennis, Clara. *Down in Nova Scotia: My Own, My Native Land.* Toronto: The Ryerson Press, 1934.

Denton, A. Leslie. *Jerome—The Man Without Legs.* Queens County Historical Society, 1982.

Deveau, J. Alphonse. *Along the Shores of Saint Mary's Bay: The Story of a Unique Community.* Vol. 2, *The Second Hundred Years.* Church Point: Imprimerie De L'Universite Sainte-Anne, 1977.

DeMont, John. "The Unsolved Tale of Silent Jerome." *Barometer,* June 21, 1979, page 19.

Ensor, Geraldine Leneika. Interview in *Elder Transcripts Project.* The Municipality of the District of Digby and the Government of Canada Millennium Partnership Fund. http://www.municipalities.com/elders/elder_sandycove.htm

Finnan, Mark. *Oak Island Secrets.* Halifax: Formac Publishing, 2002.

Haliburton, Thomas C. *History of Nova Scotia.* Vol. 1. Halifax: Printed & Published by Joseph Howe, 1829.

Hocking, Charles, FLA. *Dictionary of Disasters at Sea During the Age of Steam Including Sailing Ships and Ships of War Lost in Action, 1824-1962.* Vol. 1. London: Lloyd's Register of Shipping, 1969.

Inglesant, David, ed. *The Prisoners of Voronesh: The Diary of Sergeant George Newman.* Surrey: Unwin Brothers Limited, and the Trustees of the Regimental Museum of The Royal Welch Fusiliers. The Gresham Press, 1977.

Lawson, J. Murray. *Yarmouth Past and Present: A Book of Reminiscences.* Yarmouth: Printed and bound at the *Yarmouth Herald* office, 1902.

McCullough, Edwina Elizabeth. Quoted in *Digby Neck in Stories.* Canada's Digital Collection Program, Industry Canada. http://collections.ic.gc.ca/ digby neck/intro.htm

McGrand, Dr. Frederic Addison. *Backward Glances on Sunbury and Queens Counties.* Published by the New Brunswick Historical Society, 1967.

Obituary of Alfred William Savary, *Digby Courier*, April 1, 1920.

Obituary of Olivia Savary, *Digby Courier*, October 21, 1898.

Powell, R. Baden. *Second Scrap Book: Digby Town and Municipality.* Digby: Wallis Print, 1973.

Sacks, Dr. Oliver. *A Leg to Stand On.* New York: Summit Books, 1984.

Sacks, Dr. Oliver. *The Man Who Mistook His Wife for a Hat.* New York: Harper and Row, 1970.

Sauer, Julia Lina. *Fog Magic.* New York: Viking Penguin, 1943.

Savary, Alfred William. January 25, 1907. Annapolis Royal (Nova Scotia), Nova Scotia Archives microfilm collection: MG 100, Vol. 169.

Sherwood, Roland. "Master Storyteller," *Sagas of the Land and Sea.* Hantsport: Lancelot Press, 1980.

Sinclair, Andrew. *The Discovery of the Grail.* London: Arrow Books Ltd., 1998.

Smith, Lilah Bird. "The Mystery Man of Clare," *The Nova Scotia Historical Quarterly* 9, no. 4 (1979): 316.

Stewart, W. B., MD, FRCP(C). *Medicine in New Brunswick—A history of the practice of medicine in the Province of New Brunswick.* Saint John: New Brunswick Medical Society, printed by the Moncton Publishing Company, 1974.

Wilson, Isaiah W. *Geography and History of the County of Digby.* Halifax: Holloway Bros., 1900.

Zinck, Jack. *Shipwrecks of Nova Scotia,* Vol. 1. Windsor: Lancelot Press, 1975.

Painting of the Cunard Line steamer RMS America, *by the artist known only as "Avery." The painting depicts the ship smashing through the ice in February 1859, one of the rare winters when normally ice-free Halifax Harbour was frozen over. In the background are a number of ships docked at the Halifax wharves. Could one of these ships have on board the man who would become famous as Jerome?* (Maritime Museum of the Atlantic)

Illustration of Jerome by famed Halifax Herald *cartoonist Bob Chambers. The drawing appeared in* Down East: More Tales Told Under the Old Town Clock *(1945), by Colonel William C. Borrett. Note the dark hair and moustache.* (Anita Chambers, Estate of Robert Chambers)

Beach at Sandy Cove, with a view from the hill overlooking the beach. A similar scene would have greeted Collie Albright in 1863. (Fraser Mooney)

The home where Jerome lived and died, originally built by Dedier Comeau.
(Fraser Mooney)

Jerome monument and interpretive sign, Meteghan cemetery. (Fraser Mooney)